THE STUDENT'S
LITERARY TOOLKIT

The Most Dangerous Game
Richard Connell

The Story of an Hour
Kate Chopin

The Garden Party
Katherine Mansfield

MASTERPIECES UNVEILED

CAEZIK ACADEMIC

THIS TOOLKIT IS ALSO AVAILABLE AS A WORKBOOK

www.ArcManorBooks.com/academic
(please use lower case 'a' in academic)

Online samples
Desk copy/sample requests
Sample downloads
Custom book requests
Deep discounts for direct orders (minimum 100 copies)

ISBN: 978-1-64710-112-1

First Edition. First Printing.
September 2024
1 2 3 4 5 6 7 8 9 10

An imprint of Arc Manor

Contents

SECTION ONE

Text and Discussion Activities

The Most Dangerous Game

by Richard Connell (1924)

"**OFF** there to the right—somewhere—is a large island," said Whitney. "It's rather a mystery—"

"What island is it?" Rainsford asked.

"The old charts call it 'Ship-Trap Island,'" Whitney replied.[1] "A suggestive name, isn't it? Sailors have a curious dread of the place. I don't know why. Some superstition—"

"Can't see it," remarked Rainsford, trying to peer through the dank tropical night that was palpable as it pressed its thick warm blackness in upon the yacht.[2]

"You've good eyes," said Whitney, with a laugh, "and I've seen you pick off a moose moving in the brown fall bush at four hundred yards, but even you can't see four miles or so through a moonless Caribbean night."

"Nor four yards," admitted Rainsford. "Ugh! It's like moist black velvet."

"It will be light enough in Rio," promised Whitney. "We should make it in a few days. I hope the jaguar guns have come from Purdey's.[3] We should have some good hunting up the Amazon. Great sport, hunting."

3

"The best sport in the world," agreed Rainsford.[4]

"For the hunter," amended Whitney. "Not for the jaguar."[5]

"Don't talk rot, Whitney," said Rainsford. "You're a big-game hunter, not a philosopher. Who cares how a jaguar feels?"[6]

"Perhaps the jaguar does," observed Whitney.

"Bah! They've no understanding."

"Even so, I rather think they understand one thing—fear. The fear of pain and the fear of death."

"Nonsense," laughed Rainsford. "This hot weather is making you soft, Whitney. Be a realist. The world is made up of two classes—the hunters and the huntees.[7] Luckily, you and I are hunters. Do you think we've passed that island yet?"

"I can't tell in the dark. I hope so."

"Why?" asked Rainsford.

"The place has a reputation—a bad one."

"Cannibals?" suggested Rainsford.[8]

"Hardly. Even cannibals wouldn't live in such a God-forsaken place. But it's gotten into sailor lore, somehow. Didn't you notice that the crew's nerves seemed a bit jumpy today?"

"They were a bit strange, now you mention it. Even Captain Nielsen—"

"Yes, even that tough-minded old Swede, who'd go up to the devil himself and ask him for a light. Those fishy blue eyes held a look I never saw there before. All I could get out of him was 'This place has an evil name among seafaring men, sir.' Then he said to me, very gravely, 'Don't you feel anything?'—as if the air about us was actually poisonous. Now, you mustn't laugh when I tell you this—I did feel something like a sudden chill.

"There was no breeze. The sea was as flat as a plate-glass window. We were drawing near the island then. What I felt was a—a mental chill; a sort of sudden dread."

"Pure imagination," said Rainsford.

"One superstitious sailor can taint the whole ship's company with his fear."

"Maybe. But sometimes I think sailors have an extra sense that tells them when they are in danger. Sometimes I think evil is a tangible thing—with wave lengths, just as sound and light have.[9] An evil place can, so to speak, broadcast vibrations of evil. Anyhow, I'm glad we're getting out of this zone. Well, I think I'll turn in now, Rainsford."

"I'm not sleepy," said Rainsford. "I'm going to smoke another pipe up on the afterdeck."

"Good night, then, Rainsford. See you at breakfast."

"Right. Good night, Whitney."

There was no sound in the night as Rainsford sat there but the muffled throb of the engine that drove the yacht swiftly through the darkness, and the swish and ripple of the wash of the propeller.

Rainsford, reclining in a steamer chair, indolently puffed on his favorite brier. The sensuous drowsiness of the night was on him. "It's so dark," he thought, "that I could sleep without closing my eyes; the night would be my eyelids—"

An abrupt sound startled him. Off to the right he heard it, and his ears, expert in such matters, could not be mistaken. Again he heard the sound, and again. Somewhere, off in the blackness, someone had fired a gun three times.

Rainsford sprang up and moved quickly to the rail, mystified. He strained his eyes in the direction from which the reports had come, but it was like trying to see through a blanket. He leaped upon the rail and balanced himself there, to get greater elevation; his pipe, striking a rope, was knocked from his mouth. He lunged for it; a short, hoarse cry came from his lips as he realized he had reached too far and had lost his balance. The cry was pinched off short as the blood-warm waters of the Caribbean Sea dosed over his head.[10]

He struggled up to the surface and tried to cry out, but the wash from the speeding yacht slapped him in the face and the salt water in his open mouth made him gag and strangle. Desperately he struck out with strong strokes after the receding lights of the yacht, but he stopped before he had swum fifty feet. A certain coolheadedness had come to him; it was not the first time he had been in a tight place. There was a chance that his cries could be heard by someone aboard the yacht, but that chance was slender and grew more slender as the yacht raced on. He wrestled himself out of his clothes and shouted with all his power. The lights of the yacht became faint and ever-vanishing fireflies; then they were blotted out entirely by the night.

Rainsford remembered the shots. They had come from the right, and doggedly he swam in that direction, swimming with slow, deliberate strokes, conserving his strength. For a seemingly endless time he fought the sea. He began to count his strokes; he could do possibly a hundred more and then—

Rainsford heard a sound. It came out of the darkness, a high screaming sound, the sound of an animal in an extremity of anguish and terror.

He did not recognize the animal that made the sound; he did not try to;[11] with fresh vitality he swam toward the sound. He heard it again; then it was cut short by another noise, crisp, staccato.

"Pistol shot," muttered Rainsford, swimming on.

Ten minutes of determined effort brought another sound to his ears—the most welcome he had ever heard—the muttering and growling of the sea breaking on a rocky shore. He was almost on the rocks before he saw them; on a night less calm he would have been shattered against them. With his remaining strength he dragged himself from the swirling waters. Jagged crags appeared to jut up into the opaqueness;

he forced himself upward, hand over hand. Gasping, his hands raw, he reached a flat place at the top. Dense jungle came down to the very edge of the cliffs. What perils that tangle of trees and underbrush might hold for him did not concern Rainsford just then. All he knew was that he was safe from his enemy, the sea, and that utter weariness was on him. He flung himself down at the jungle edge and tumbled headlong into the deepest sleep of his life.[12]

When he opened his eyes he knew from the position of the sun that it was late in the afternoon. Sleep had given him new vigor; a sharp hunger was picking at him. He looked about him, almost cheerfully.

"Where there are pistol shots, there are men. Where there are men, there is food," he thought. But what kind of men, he wondered, in so forbidding a place? An unbroken front of snarled and ragged jungle fringed the shore.

He saw no sign of a trail through the closely knit web of weeds and trees; it was easier to go along the shore, and Rainsford floundered along by the water. Not far from where he landed, he stopped.

Some wounded thing—by the evidence, a large animal—had thrashed about in the underbrush; the jungle weeds were crushed down and the moss was lacerated; one patch of weeds was stained crimson. A small, glittering object not far away caught Rainsford's eye and he picked it up. It was an empty cartridge.

"A twenty-two," he remarked. "That's odd. It must have been a fairly large animal too. The hunter had his nerve with him to tackle it with a light gun. It's clear that the brute put up a fight. I suppose the first three shots I heard was when the hunter flushed his quarry and wounded it. The last shot was when he trailed it here and finished it."

He examined the ground closely and found what he had hoped to find—the print of hunting boots. They pointed along the cliff in the direction he had been going. Eagerly he hurried along, now slipping on a rotten log or a loose stone, but making headway; night was beginning to settle down on the island.

Bleak darkness was blacking out the sea and jungle when Rainsford sighted the lights. He came upon them as he turned a crook in the coast line; and his first thought was that be had come upon a village, for there were many lights. But as he forged along he saw to his great astonishment that all the lights were in one enormous building—a lofty structure with pointed towers plunging upward into the gloom. His eyes made out the shadowy outlines of a palatial chateau; it was set on a high bluff, and on three sides of it cliffs dived down to where the sea licked greedy lips in the shadows.

"Mirage," thought Rainsford. But it was no mirage, he found, when he opened the tall spiked iron gate. The stone steps were real enough; the massive door with a leering gargoyle for a knocker was real enough; yet above it all hung an air of unreality.

He lifted the knocker, and it creaked up stiffly, as if it had never before been used. He let it fall, and it startled him with its booming loudness. He thought he heard steps within; the door remained closed. Again Rainsford lifted the heavy knocker, and let it fall. The door opened then—opened as suddenly as if it were on a spring—and Rainsford stood blinking in the river of glaring gold light that poured out. The first thing Rainsford's eyes discerned was the largest man Rainsford had ever seen—a gigantic creature, solidly made and black bearded to the waist. In his hand the man held a long-barreled revolver, and he was pointing it straight at Rainsford's heart.

Out of the snarl of beard two small eyes regarded Rainsford.

"Don't be alarmed," said Rainsford, with a smile which he hoped was disarming. "I'm no robber. I fell off a yacht. My name is Sanger Rainsford of New York City."

The menacing look in the eyes did not change. The revolver pointing as rigidly as if the giant were a statue. He gave no sign that he understood Rainsford's words, or that he had even heard them. He was dressed in uniform—a black uniform trimmed with gray astrakhan.

"I'm Sanger Rainsford of New York," Rainsford began again. "I fell off a yacht. I am hungry."

The man's only answer was to raise with his thumb the hammer of his revolver. Then Rainsford saw the man's free hand go to his forehead in a military salute, and he saw him click his heels together and stand at attention. Another man was coming down the broad marble steps, an erect, slender man in evening clothes. He advanced to Rainsford and held out his hand.

In a cultivated voice marked by a slight accent that gave it added precision and deliberateness, he said, "It is a very great pleasure and honor to welcome Mr. Sanger Rainsford, the celebrated hunter, to my home."

Automatically Rainsford shook the man's hand.

"I've read your book about hunting snow leopards in Tibet, you see," explained the man. "I am General Zaroff."

Rainsford's first impression was that the man was singularly handsome; his second was that there was an original, almost bizarre quality about the general's face. He was a tall man past middle age, for his hair was a vivid white; but his thick eyebrows and pointed military mustache were as black as the night from which Rainsford had come. His eyes, too, were black and very bright. He had high cheekbones, a sharpcut nose, a spare, dark face—the face of a man used to giving orders, the face of an aristocrat.[13] Turning to the giant in uniform, the general made a sign. The giant put away his pistol, saluted, withdrew.

"Ivan is an incredibly strong fellow," remarked the general, "but he has the misfortune to be deaf and dumb. A simple fellow, but, I'm afraid, like all his race, a bit of a savage."

"Is he Russian?"

"He is a Cossack," said the general, and his smile showed red lips and pointed teeth.[14] "So am I."

"Come," he said, "we shouldn't be chatting here. We can talk later. Now you want clothes, food, rest. You shall have them. This is a most-restful spot."

Ivan had reappeared, and the general spoke to him with lips that moved but gave forth no sound.

"Follow Ivan, if you please, Mr. Rainsford," said the general. "I was about to have my dinner when you came. I'll wait for you. You'll find that my clothes will fit you, I think."

It was to a huge, beam-ceilinged bedroom with a canopied bed big enough for six men that Rainsford followed the silent giant. Ivan laid out an evening suit, and Rainsford, as he put it on, noticed that it came from a London tailor who ordinarily cut and sewed for none below the rank of duke.

The dining room to which Ivan conducted him was in many ways remarkable. There was a medieval magnificence about it; it suggested a baronial hall of feudal times with its oaken panels, its high ceiling, its vast refectory tables where twoscore men could sit down to eat.[15] About the hall were mounted heads of many animals—lions, tigers, elephants, moose, bears; larger or more perfect specimens Rainsford had never seen.[16] At the great table the general was sitting, alone.

"You'll have a cocktail, Mr. Rainsford," he suggested. The cocktail was surpassingly good; and, Rainsford noted, the table appointments were of the finest—the linen, the crystal, the silver, the china.

They were eating borsch, the rich, red soup with whipped cream so dear to Russian palates. Half apologetically General Zaroff said, "We do our best to preserve the amenities of civilization here. Please forgive any lapses. We are well off the beaten track, you know. Do you think the champagne has suffered from its long ocean trip?"

"Not in the least," declared Rainsford. He was finding the general a most thoughtful and affable host, a true cosmopolite. But there was one small trait of the general's that made Rainsford uncomfortable. Whenever he looked up from his plate he found the general studying him, appraising him narrowly.

"Perhaps," said General Zaroff, "you were surprised that I recognized your name. You see, I read all books on hunting published in English, French, and Russian. I have but one passion in my life, Mr. Rainsford, and it is the hunt."[17]

"You have some wonderful heads here," said Rainsford as he ate a particularly well-cooked filet mignon. "That Cape buffalo is the largest I ever saw."

"Oh, that fellow. Yes, he was a monster."

"Did he charge you?"

"Hurled me against a tree," said the general. "Fractured my skull. But I got the brute."

"I've always thought," said Rainsford, "that the Cape buffalo is the most dangerous of all big game."

For a moment the general did not reply; he was smiling his curious red-lipped smile. Then he said slowly, "No. You are wrong, sir. The Cape buffalo is not the most dangerous big game." He sipped his wine. "Here in my preserve on this island," he said in the same slow tone, "I hunt more dangerous game."

Rainsford expressed his surprise. "Is there big game on this island?"

The general nodded. "The biggest."

"Really?"

"Oh, it isn't here naturally, of course. I have to stock the island."[18]

"What have you imported, general?" Rainsford asked. "Tigers?"

The general smiled. "No," he said. "Hunting tigers ceased to interest me some years ago. I exhausted their possibilities, you see. No thrill left in tigers, no real danger. I live for danger, Mr. Rainsford."

The general took from his pocket a gold cigarette case and offered his guest a long black cigarette with a silver tip; it was perfumed and gave off a smell like incense.

"We will have some capital hunting, you and I," said the general. "I shall be most glad to have your society."

"But what game—" began Rainsford.

"I'll tell you," said the general. "You will be amused, I know. I think I may say, in all modesty, that I have done a rare thing. I have invented a new sensation. May I pour you another glass of port?"

"Thank you, general."

The general filled both glasses, and said, "God makes some men poets. Some He makes kings, some beggars. Me He made a hunter.[19] My hand was made for the trigger, my father said. He was a very rich man with a quarter of a million acres in the Crimea, and he was an ardent sportsman. When I was only five years old he gave me a little gun, specially made in Moscow for me, to shoot sparrows with. When I shot some of his prize turkeys with it, he did not punish me; he complimented me on my marksmanship. I killed my first bear in the Caucasus when I was ten. My whole life has been one prolonged hunt. I went into the army—it was expected of noblemen's sons—and for a time commanded a division of Cossack cavalry, but my real interest was always the hunt. I have hunted every kind of game in every land. It would be impossible for me to tell you how many animals I have killed."

The general puffed at his cigarette.

"After the debacle in Russia I left the country, for it was imprudent for an officer of the Czar to stay there.[20] Many noble Russians lost everything. I, luckily, had invested heavily in American securities, so I shall never have to open a tearoom in Monte Carlo or drive a taxi in Paris. Naturally, I continued to hunt—grizzliest in your Rockies, crocodiles in the Ganges, rhinoceroses in East Africa. It was in Africa that the Cape buffalo hit me and laid me up for six months. As soon as I recovered I started for the Amazon to hunt jaguars, for I had heard they were unusually cunning. They weren't." The Cossack sighed. "They were no match at all for a hunter with his wits about him, and a high-powered rifle. I was bitterly disappointed. I was lying in my tent with a splitting headache one night when a terrible thought pushed its way into my mind. Hunting was beginning to bore me! And hunting, remember, had been my life. I have heard that in America businessmen often go to pieces when they give up the business that has been their life."

"Yes, that's so," said Rainsford.

The general smiled. "I had no wish to go to pieces," he said. "I must do something. Now, mine is an analytical mind, Mr. Rainsford. Doubtless that is why I enjoy the problems of the chase."

"No doubt, General Zaroff."

"So," continued the general, "I asked myself why the hunt no longer fascinated me. You are much younger than I am, Mr. Rainsford, and have not hunted as much, but you perhaps can guess the answer."

"What was it?"

"Simply this: hunting had ceased to be what you call 'a sporting proposition.' It had become too easy. I always got my quarry. Always. There is no greater bore than perfection."

The general lit a fresh cigarette.

"No animal had a chance with me any more. That is no boast; it is a mathematical certainty. The animal had nothing but his legs and his instinct. Instinct is no match for reason. When I thought of this it was a tragic moment for me, I can tell you."

Rainsford leaned across the table, absorbed in what his host was saying.

"It came to me as an inspiration what I must do," the general went on.

"And that was?"

The general smiled the quiet smile of one who has faced an obstacle and surmounted it with success. "I had to invent a new animal to hunt," he said.

"A new animal? You're joking."

"Not at all," said the general. "I never joke about hunting. I needed a new animal. I found one. So I bought this island built this house, and here I do my hunting. The island is perfect for my purposes—there are jungles with a maze of traits in them, hills, swamps—"[21]

"But the animal, General Zaroff?"

"Oh," said the general, "it supplies me with the most exciting hunting in the world. No other hunting compares with it for an instant. Every day I hunt, and I never grow bored now, for I have a quarry with which I can match my wits."

Rainsford's bewilderment showed in his face.

"I wanted the ideal animal to hunt," explained the general. "So I said, 'What are the attributes of an ideal quarry?' And the answer was, of course, 'It must have courage, cunning, and, above all, it must be able to reason.'"

"But no animal can reason," objected Rainsford.

"My dear fellow," said the general, "there is one that can."

"But you can't mean—" gasped Rainsford.

"And why not?"

"I can't believe you are serious, General Zaroff. This is a grisly joke."

"Why should I not be serious? I am speaking of hunting."

"Hunting? Great Guns, General Zaroff, what you speak of is murder."[22]

The general laughed with entire good nature. He regarded Rainsford quizzically. "I refuse to believe that so modern and civilized a young man as you seem to be harbors romantic ideas about the value of human life.[23] Surely your experiences in the war—"[24]

"Did not make me condone cold-blooded murder," finished Rainsford stiffly.

Laughter shook the general. "How extraordinarily droll you are!" he said. "One does not expect nowadays to find a young man of the educated class, even in America, with such a naive, and, if I may say so, mid-Victorian point of view.[25] It's like finding a snuffbox in a limousine. Ah, well, doubtless you had Puritan ancestors. So many Americans appear to have had. I'll wager you'll forget your notions when you go hunting with me. You've a genuine new thrill in store for you, Mr. Rainsford."

"Thank you, I'm a hunter, not a murderer."

"Dear me," said the general, quite unruffled, "again that unpleasant word. But I think I can show you that your scruples are quite ill founded."

"Yes?"

"Life is for the strong, to be lived by the strong, and, if needs be, taken by the strong. The weak of the world were put here to give the strong pleasure. I am strong. Why should I not use my gift? If I wish to hunt, why should I not? I hunt the scum of the earth: sailors from tramp ships—lassars, blacks, Chinese, whites, mongrels—a thoroughbred horse or hound is worth more than a score of them."

"But they are men," said Rainsford hotly.

"Precisely," said the general. "That is why I use them. It gives me pleasure. They can reason, after a fashion. So they are dangerous."

"But where do you get them?"

The general's left eyelid fluttered down in a wink. "This island is called Ship Trap," he answered. "Sometimes an angry god of the high seas sends them to me. Sometimes, when Providence is not so kind, I help Providence a bit. Come to the window with me."

Rainsford went to the window and looked out toward the sea.

"Watch! Out there!" exclaimed the general, pointing into the night. Rainsford's eyes saw only blackness, and then, as the general pressed a button, far out to sea Rainsford saw the flash of lights.

The general chuckled. "They indicate a channel," he said, "where there's none; giant rocks with razor edges crouch like a sea monster with wide-open jaws. They can crush a ship as easily as I crush this nut." He dropped a walnut on the hardwood floor and brought his heel grinding down on it. "Oh, yes," he said, casually, as if in answer to a question, "I have electricity. We try to be civilized here."

"Civilized?[26] And you shoot down men?"

A trace of anger was in the general's black eyes, but it was there for but a second; and he said, in his most pleasant manner, "Dear me, what a righteous young man you are! I assure you I do not do the thing you suggest. That would be barbarous. I treat these visitors with every consideration. They get plenty of good food and exercise. They get into splendid physical condition. You shall see for yourself tomorrow."

"What do you mean?"

"We'll visit my training school," smiled the general. "It's in the cellar. I have about a dozen pupils down there now. They're from the Spanish bark San Lucar that had the bad luck to go on the rocks out there. A very inferior lot, I regret to say. Poor specimens and more accustomed to the deck than to the jungle."[27] He raised his hand, and Ivan, who served as waiter, brought thick Turkish coffee. Rainsford, with an effort, held his tongue in check.

"It's a game, you see," pursued the general blandly. "I suggest to one of them that we go hunting. I give him a supply of food and an excellent hunting knife. I give him three hours' start. I am to follow, armed only with a pistol of the smallest caliber and range. If my quarry eludes me for three whole days, he wins the game. If I find him"—the general smiled—"he loses."

"Suppose he refuses to be hunted?"

"Oh," said the general, "I give him his option, of course. He need not play that game if he doesn't wish to. If he does not wish to hunt, I turn him over to Ivan. Ivan once had the honor of serving as official knouter to the Great White Czar, and he has his own ideas of sport. Invariably, Mr. Rainsford, invariably they choose the hunt."

"And if they win?"

The smile on the general's face widened. "To date I have not lost," he said. Then he added, hastily: "I don't wish you to think me a braggart, Mr. Rainsford. Many of them afford only the most elementary sort of problem. Occasionally I strike a tartar. One almost did win. I eventually had to use the dogs."

"The dogs?"

"This way, please. I'll show you."

The general steered Rainsford to a window. The lights from the windows sent a flickering illumination that made grotesque patterns on the courtyard below, and Rainsford could see moving about there a dozen or so huge black shapes; as they turned toward him, their eyes glittered greenly.

"A rather good lot, I think," observed the general. "They are let out at seven every night. If anyone should try to get into my house—or out of it—something extremely regrettable would occur to him." He hummed a snatch of song from the Folies Bergere.

"And now," said the general, "I want to show you my new collection of heads. Will you come with me to the library?"

"I hope," said Rainsford, "that you will excuse me tonight, General Zaroff. I'm really not feeling well."

"Ah, indeed?" the general inquired solicitously. "Well, I suppose that's only natural, after your long swim. You need a good, restful night's sleep. Tomorrow you'll feel like a new man, I'll wager. Then we'll hunt, eh? I've one rather promising prospect—" Rainsford was hurrying from the room.

"Sorry you can't go with me tonight," called the general. "I expect rather fair sport—a big, strong, black.[28] He looks resourceful— Well, good night, Mr. Rainsford; I hope you have a good night's rest."

The bed was good, and the pajamas of the softest silk, and he was tired in every fiber of his being, but nevertheless Rainsford could not quiet his brain with the opiate of sleep. He lay, eyes wide open. Once he thought he heard stealthy steps in the corridor outside his room. He sought to throw open the door; it would not open. He went to the window and looked out. His room was high up in one of the towers. The lights of the chateau were out now, and it was dark and silent; but there was a fragment of sallow moon, and by its wan light he could see, dimly, the courtyard. There, weaving in and out in the pattern of shadow, were black, noiseless forms; the hounds heard him at the window and looked up, expectantly, with their green eyes. Rainsford went back to the bed and lay down. By many methods he tried to put himself to sleep. He had achieved a doze when, just as morning began to come, he heard, far off in the jungle, the faint report of a pistol.

General Zaroff did not appear until luncheon. He was dressed faultlessly in the tweeds of a country squire. He was solicitous about the state of Rainsford's health.

"As for me," sighed the general, "I do not feel so well. I am worried, Mr. Rainsford. Last night I detected traces of my old complaint."

To Rainsford's questioning glance the general said, "Ennui. Boredom."

Then, taking a second helping of crepes Suzette, the general explained: "The hunting was not good last night. The fellow lost his head. He made a straight trail that offered no problems at all. That's the trouble with these sailors; they have dull brains to begin with, and they do not know how to get about in the woods. They do excessively stupid and obvious things. It's most annoying. Will you have another glass of Chablis, Mr. Rainsford?"

"General," said Rainsford firmly, "I wish to leave this island at once."

The general raised his thickets of eyebrows; he seemed hurt. "But, my dear fellow," the general protested, "you've only just come. You've had no hunting—"

"I wish to go today," said Rainsford. He saw the dead black eyes of the general on him, studying him. General Zaroff's face suddenly brightened.

He filled Rainsford's glass with venerable Chablis from a dusty bottle.

"Tonight," said the general, "we will hunt—you and I."

Rainsford shook his head. "No, general," he said. "I will not hunt."

The general shrugged his shoulders and delicately ate a hothouse grape. "As you wish, my friend," he said. "The choice rests entirely with you. But may I not venture to suggest that you will find my idea of sport more diverting than Ivan's?"

He nodded toward the corner to where the giant stood, scowling, his thick arms crossed on his hogshead of chest.

"You don't mean—" cried Rainsford.

"My dear fellow," said the general, "have I not told you I always mean what I say about hunting? This is really an inspiration. I drink to a foeman worthy of my steel—at last." The general raised his glass, but Rainsford sat staring at him.

"You'll find this game worth playing," the general said enthusiastically. "Your brain against mine. Your woodcraft against mine. Your strength and stamina against mine. Outdoor chess! And the stake is not without value, eh?"

"And if I win—" began Rainsford huskily.

"I'll cheerfully acknowledge myself defeat if I do not find you by midnight of the third day," said General Zaroff. "My sloop will place you on the mainland near a town." The general read what Rainsford was thinking.

"Oh, you can trust me," said the Cossack. "I will give you my word as a gentleman and a sportsman. Of course you, in turn, must agree to say nothing of your visit here."[29]

"I'll agree to nothing of the kind," said Rainsford.

"Oh," said the general, "in that case— But why discuss that now? Three days hence we can discuss it over a bottle of Veuve Cliquot, unless—"

The general sipped his wine.

Then a businesslike air animated him. "Ivan," he said to Rainsford, "will supply you with hunting clothes, food, a knife. I suggest you wear moccasins; they leave a poorer trail. I suggest, too, that you avoid the big swamp in the southeast corner of the island. We call it Death Swamp.

There's quicksand there. One foolish fellow tried it. The deplorable part of it was that Lazarus followed him. You can imagine my feelings, Mr. Rainsford. I loved Lazarus; he was the finest hound in my pack.[30] Well, I must beg you to excuse me now. I always take a siesta after lunch. You'll hardly have time for a nap, I fear. You'll want to start, no doubt. I shall not follow till dusk. Hunting at night is so much more exciting than by day, don't you think? Au revoir, Mr. Rainsford, au revoir." General Zaroff, with a deep, courtly bow, strolled from the room.

From another door came Ivan. Under one arm he carried khaki hunting clothes, a haversack of food, a leather sheath containing a long-bladed hunting knife; his right hand rested on a cocked revolver thrust in the crimson sash about his waist.

Rainsford had fought his way through the bush for two hours. "I must keep my nerve. I must keep my nerve," he said through tight teeth.

He had not been entirely clearheaded when the chateau gates snapped shut behind him. His whole idea at first was to put distance between himself and General Zaroff; and, to this end, he had plunged along, spurred on by the sharp rowers of something very like panic. Now he had got a grip on himself, had stopped, and was taking stock of himself and the situation. He saw that straight flight was futile; inevitably it would bring him face to face with the sea. He was in a picture with a frame of water, and his operations, clearly, must take place within that frame.

"I'll give him a trail to follow," muttered Rainsford, and he struck off from the rude path he had been following into the trackless wilderness. He executed a series of intricate loops; he doubled on his trail again and again, recalling all the lore of the fox hunt, and all the dodges of the fox. Night found him leg-weary, with hands and face lashed by the branches, on a thickly wooded ridge. He knew it would be insane to blunder on through the dark, even if he had the strength. His need for rest was imperative and he thought, "I have played the fox, now I must play the cat of the fable." A big tree with a thick trunk and outspread branches was near by, and, taking care to leave not the slightest mark, he climbed up into the crotch, and, stretching out on one of the broad limbs, after a fashion, rested. Rest brought him new confidence and almost a feeling of security. Even so zealous a hunter as General Zaroff could not trace him there, he told himself; only the devil himself could follow that complicated trail through the jungle after dark. But perhaps the general was a devil—

An apprehensive night crawled slowly by like a wounded snake and sleep did not visit Rainsford, although the silence of a dead world was on the jungle. Toward morning when a dingy gray was varnishing the sky, the cry of some startled bird focused Rainsford's attention in that direction. Something was coming through the bush, coming slowly, carefully, coming by the same winding way Rainsford had come. He flattened himself down on the limb and, through a screen of leaves almost as thick as tapestry, he watched ....That which was approaching was a man.

It was General Zaroff. He made his way along with his eyes fixed in utmost concentration on the ground before him. He paused, almost beneath the tree, dropped to his knees and studied the ground. Rainsford's impulse was to hurl himself down like a panther, but he saw that the general's right hand held something metallic—a small automatic pistol.

The hunter shook his head several times, as if he were puzzled. Then he straightened up and took from his case one of his black cigarettes; its pungent incense like smoke floated up to Rainsford's nostrils.

Rainsford held his breath. The general's eyes had left the ground and were traveling inch by inch up the tree. Rainsford froze there, every muscle tensed for a spring. But the sharp eyes of the hunter stopped before they reached the limb where Rainsford lay; a smile spread over his brown face. Very deliberately he blew a smoke ring into the air; then he turned his back on the tree and walked carelessly away, back along the trail he had come. The swish of the underbrush against his hunting boots grew fainter and fainter.

The pent-up air burst hotly from Rainsford's lungs. His first thought made him feel sick and numb. The general could follow a trail through the woods at night; he could follow an extremely difficult trail; he must have uncanny powers; only by the merest chance had the Cossack failed to see his quarry.

Rainsford's second thought was even more terrible. It sent a shudder of cold horror through his whole being. Why had the general smiled? Why had he turned back?

Rainsford did not want to believe what his reason told him was true, but the truth was as evident as the sun that had by now pushed through the morning mists. The general was playing with him! The general was saving him for another day's sport! The Cossack was the cat; he was the mouse. Then it was that Rainsford knew the full meaning of terror.[31]

"I will not lose my nerve. I will not."

He slid down from the tree, and struck off again into the woods. His face was set and he forced the machinery of his mind to function. Three hundred yards from his hiding place he stopped where a huge dead tree leaned precariously on a smaller, living one. Throwing off his sack of food, Rainsford took his knife from its sheath and began to work with all his energy.

The job was finished at last, and he threw himself down behind a fallen log a hundred feet away. He did not have to wait long. The cat was coming again to play with the mouse. Following the trail with the sureness of a bloodhound came General Zaroff.[32] Nothing escaped those searching black eyes, no crushed blade of grass, no bent twig, no mark, no matter how faint, in the moss. So intent was the Cossack on his stalking that he was upon the thing Rainsford had made before he saw it. His foot touched the protruding bough that was the trigger. Even as he touched it, the general sensed his danger and leped back with the agility of an ape. But he was not quite quick enough; the dead tree, delicately adjusted to rest on the cut living one, crashed down and struck the general a glancing blow on the shoulder as it fell; but for his alertness, he must have been smashed beneath it. He staggered, but he did not fall; nor did he drop his revolver. He stood there, rubbing his injured shoulder, and Rainsford, with fear again gripping his heart, heard the general's mocking laugh ring through the jungle.

"Rainsford," called the general, "if you are within sound of my voice, as I suppose you are, let me congratulate you. Not many men know how to make a Malay mancatcher. Luckily for me I, too, have hunted in Malacca. You are proving interesting, Mr. Rainsford. I am going now to have my wound dressed; it's only a slight one. But I shall be back. I shall be back."

When the general, nursing his bruised shoulder, had gone, Rainsford took up his flight again. It was flight now, a desperate, hopeless flight, that carried him on for some hours. Dusk came, then darkness, and still he pressed on. The ground grew softer under his moccasins; the vegetation grew ranker, denser; insects bit him savagely.

Then, as he stepped forward, his foot sank into the ooze. He tried to wrench it back, but the muck sucked viciously at his foot as if it were a giant leech. With a violent effort, he tore his feet loose. He knew where he was now. Death Swamp and its quicksand.

His hands were tight closed as if his nerve were something tangible that someone in the darkness was trying to tear from his grip. The softness of the earth had given him an idea. He stepped back from the quicksand a dozen feet or so and, like some huge prehistoric beaver, he began to dig.

Rainsford had dug himself in in France when a second's delay meant death. That had been a placid pastime compared to his digging now. The pit grew deeper; when it was above his shoulders, he climbed out and from some hard saplings cut stakes and sharpened them to a fine point. These stakes he planted in the bottom of the pit with the points sticking up. With flying fingers he wove a rough carpet of weeds and branches and with it he covered the mouth of the pit. Then, wet with sweat and aching with tiredness, he crouched behind the stump of a lightning-charred tree.

He knew his pursuer was coming; he heard the padding sound of feet on the soft earth, and the night breeze brought him the perfume of the general's cigarette. It seemed to Rainsford that the general was coming with unusual swiftness; he was not feeling his way along, foot by foot. Rainsford, crouching there, could not see the general, nor could he see the pit. He lived a year in a minute. Then he felt an impulse to cry aloud with joy, for he heard the sharp crackle of the breaking branches as the cover of the pit gave way; he heard the sharp scream of pain as the pointed stakes found their mark. He leaped up from his place of concealment. Then he cowered back. Three feet from the pit a man was standing, with an electric torch in his hand.

"You've done well, Rainsford," the voice of the general called. "Your Burmese tiger pit has claimed one of my best dogs. Again you score. I think, Mr. Rainsford, I'll see what you can do against my whole pack. I'm going home for a rest now. Thank you for a most amusing evening."

At daybreak Rainsford, lying near the swamp, was awakened by a sound that made him know that he had new things to learn about fear. It was a distant sound, faint and wavering, but he knew it. It was the baying of a pack of hounds.

Rainsford knew he could do one of two things. He could stay where he was and wait. That was suicide. He could flee. That was postponing the inevitable. For a moment he stood there, thinking. An idea that held a wild chance came to him, and, tightening his belt, he headed away from the swamp.

The baying of the hounds drew nearer, then still nearer, nearer, ever nearer. On a ridge Rainsford climbed a tree. Down a watercourse, not a quarter of a mile away, he could see the bush moving. Straining his eyes, he saw the lean figure of General Zaroff; just ahead of him Rainsford made out another figure whose wide shoulders surged through the tall jungle weeds; it was the giant Ivan, and he seemed pulled forward by some unseen force; Rainsford knew that Ivan must be holding the pack in leash.

They would be on him any minute now. His mind worked frantically. He thought of a native trick he had learned in Uganda. He slid down the tree. He caught hold of a springy young sapling and to it he fastened his hunting knife, with the blade pointing down the trail; with a bit of wild grapevine he tied back the sapling. Then he ran for his life. The hounds raised their voices as they hit the fresh scent. Rainsford knew now how an animal at bay feels.

He had to stop to get his breath. The baying of the hounds stopped abruptly, and Rainsford's heart stopped too. They must have reached the knife.

He shinned excitedly up a tree and looked back. His pursuers had stopped. But the hope that was in Rainsford's brain when he climbed died, for he saw in the shallow valley that General Zaroff was still on his feet. But Ivan was not. The knife, driven by the recoil of the springing tree, had not wholly failed.

Rainsford had hardly tumbled to the ground when the pack took up the cry again.

"Nerve, nerve, nerve!" he panted, as he dashed along. A blue gap showed between the trees dead ahead. Ever nearer drew the hounds. Rainsford forced himself on toward that gap. He reached it. It was the shore of the sea. Across a cove he could see the gloomy gray stone of the chateau. Twenty feet below him the sea rumbled and hissed. Rainsford hesitated. He heard the hounds. Then he leaped far out into the sea ....

When the general and his pack reached the place by the sea, the Cossack stopped. For some minutes he stood regarding the blue-green expanse of water. He shrugged his shoulders. Then he sat down, took a drink of brandy from a silver flask, lit a cigarette, and hummed a bit from Madame Butterfly.[33]

General Zaroff had an exceedingly good dinner in his great paneled dining hall that evening. With it he had a bottle of Pol Roger and half a bottle of Chambertin. Two slight annoyances kept him from perfect enjoyment. One was the thought that it would be difficult to replace Ivan; the other was that his quarry had escaped him; of course, the American hadn't played the game—so thought the general as he tasted his after-dinner liqueur. In his library he read, to soothe himself, from the works of Marcus Aurelius. At ten he went up to his bedroom. He was deliciously tired, he said to himself, as he locked himself in. There was a little moonlight, so, before turning on his light, he went to the window and looked down at the courtyard. He could see the great hounds, and he called, "Better luck another time," to them. Then he switched on the light.

A man, who had been hiding in the curtains of the bed, was standing there.

"Rainsford!" screamed the general. "How in God's name did you get here?"

"Swam," said Rainsford. "I found it quicker than walking through the jungle."

The general sucked in his breath and smiled. "I congratulate you," he said. "You have won the game."

Rainsford did not smile. "I am still a beast at bay," he said, in a low, hoarse voice. "Get ready, General Zaroff."

The general made one of his deepest bows. "I see," he said. "Splendid! One of us is to furnish a repast for the hounds. The other will sleep in this very excellent bed. On guard, Rainsford." …

He had never slept in a better bed, Rainsford decided.[34]

DISCUSSION QUESTIONS

1. How does the author use names throughout the story? What is the significance of General Zaroff's name, for example, or the choice of "Ship-Trap Island" and "Death Swamp" to describe certain settings?

2. What is the importance of the tropical setting to the story? Why does Connell locate the story in a tropical region and on an island?

3. Why is it Rainsford who introduces the idea of the "two classes" within the story? How does Connell play with the irony of this as the story progresses?

4. What is the importance of Rainsford's position as a famous big-game hunter? What point does Connell perhaps seek to make about the popularity of hunting in the 1920s, particularly in places like Africa?

5. What is the significance of General Zaroff's identity as a Cossack and someone who was involved in the Tsarist government of Russia before the Revolution? Why is it important that he is effectively in exile in the wake of the Russian Revolution?

6. How does Connell represent Rainsford's growing fear as he realizes that General Zaroff is hunting men and that he himself is going to be hunted? How does Rainsford's fear enhance the major themes of the story about the brutality of the "two class" system that Rainsford himself referred to?

7. How might you connect the story to the historical context of World War I? This story was published in 1924, only six years after the war's conclusion in 1918.

Although the more direct historical reference is certainly to the Russian Revolution because of General Zaroff's Cossack identity, his military status, and several other allusions within the story show Connell's acknowledgment of the war. Given the war's association with a horrendous loss of life (it was called the Great War because the devastation was unprecedented), is there a connection that Connell makes between war and a brutal disregard for human life?

8. How does Rainsford's victory over General Zaroff reinforce the message of the story? Under what circumstances do you see Rainsford having overpowered the General? Why does the author cut to the statement about Rainsford sleeping in General Zaroff's bed? Do you think that Rainsford seeks to step into the General's shoes? Will he continue the "game" on the island or shut it down? Why?

VOCABULARY ACTIVITY

1. Locate each word in the text. Use context clues to create a definition for each word.

2. Use a dictionary and write a new definition in your own words that is more accurate.

- *Amenities*
- *Elude*
- *Feudal*
- *Futile*
- *Indolent*
- *Opaque*
- *Palpable*
- *Repast*
- *Scruples*
- *Staccato*
- *Tangible*
- *Vitality*

SEMANTIC MAP

Instructions: You will create a semantic map of vocabulary words used in the story. Start by placing the assigned word in the middle of the page. Then add more information with lines that show the connections.

1. Use context clues and a dictionary to define the word.

2. Add synonyms and antonyms.

3. Include words or phrases that add to the meaning.

4. Add images that clarify the meaning. (Include image credits.)

5. Share your semantic map with other students and read theirs.

6. Use this page and the next to plan your poster-board.

CONNOTATION AND DENOTATION

Define Connotation

Define Denotation

1. Consider some of the different definitions for the word *home*.

    a. The denotation of **home**

    b. The connotation of **home**

2. The title of the story, "The Most Dangerous Game" includes a word with multiple meanings. What are some different definitions of *game*?

3. Provide an example from the text that supports the idea that *game* is a contest or sport.

4. Provide an example from the text that supports the idea that *game* is an animal that is hunted.

5. Why do you think the author chose the title "The Most Dangerous Game"? How do connotation and denotation change the meaning of the title?

6. Another set of words we should examine in "The Most Dangerous Game" are *hunting* and *murder*.
   What is the *denotation* of these two words?

    a. Hunting

    b. Murder

7. List a few examples of how Zaroff and Rainsford use these words in the text to describe the same event.

    a. Hunting

    b. Murder

8. Sometimes, the difference in the definition of words is partly due to the tone of the word, or the emotion we attach to it. For each word, is the tone *positive, negative,* or *neutral?*

   a. Hunting

   b. Murder

9. Why doesn't Zaroff like the word *murder?*

10. Explain Rainsford's position on their disagreement about the meaning of *hunting* vs *murder.*

11. How does Zaroff justify his use of the word *hunting?*

CHARACTER ANALYSIS

Authors combine the tools they use to create an engaging story. In this assignment, we will analyze the characters. However, it is important to remember that characters are a necessary part of the plot and contribute to the theme. Each of the author's tools, in this case, characterization, makes their other tools sharper. As you complete the analysis of these characters, consider what they have in common, what differs, and how their differences lead to their conflict.

Character Name: Sanger Rainsford

1. Appearance
   a. Answer in your own words
   b. Provide a quotation to support your answer

2. Background information
   a. Answer in your own words
   b. Provide a quotation to support your answer

3. Interests and values
   a. Answer in your own words
   b. Provide a quotation to support your answer

4. Why is he on the Island?
   a. Answer in your own words
   b. Provide a quotation to support your answer

5. How does he value human life?
   a. Answer in your own words
   b. Provide a quotation to support your answer

6. How does his background impact the way he values human life?

   a. Answer in your own words

   b. Provide a quotation to support your answer

Character Name: General Zaroff

1. Appearance

   a. Answer in your own words

   b. Provide a quotation to support your answer

2. Background information

   a. Answer in your own words

   b. Provide a quotation to support your answer

3. Interests and values

   a. Answer in your own words

   b. Provide a quotation to support your answer

4. Why is he on the Island?

   a. Answer in your own words

   b. Provide a quotation to support your answer

5. How does he value human life?

   a. Answer in your own words

   b. Provide a quotation to support your answer

6. How does his background impact the way he values human life?

   a. Answer in your own words

   b. Provide a quotation to support your answer

THEME ANALYSIS

Theme is a core statement of an author's message in their writing. Stories may have more than one theme deliberately included by the author, and they may generate ideas about unintended themes in the reader.

When we talk about theme in literature, sometimes we talk about a single word or short phrase that identifies the core idea in the theme. For example, If you were discussing *Romeo and Juliet*, you might say the theme is "love." When moving to writing about theme, though, we need to add more context to the idea than just one word. A strong analysis of the theme will lead to a theme statement.

1. List 3 theme words or short phrases from "The Most Dangerous Game."

2. Next, we want to create a complete sentence about the theme. Remember that the theme statement will not include specific details from the story. Use the theme "the value of human life" to create a theme statement.

   a. What does the author, Richard Connell, want the readers to think about the value of human life?

   b. Write your final theme statement here

WRITING ASSIGNMENT

Instructions: Using your notes on character, theme, setting, and context, as well as the annotated text provided, write an essay that addresses the following prompt.

How does the characterization of Rainsford and Zaroff contribute to the theme of "The Most Dangerous Game"?

The Story of an Hour

by Kate Chopin (1894)

KNOWING that Mrs. Mallard was afflicted with a heart trouble, great care was taken to break to her as gently as possible the news of her husband's death.[35] He was the one who saw Mr. Mallard's name on the list of "killed" and he also took the time to send a second telegram to ensure that.

It was her sister Josephine who told her, in broken sentences; veiled hints that revealed in half concealing.[36] Her husband's friend Richards was there, too, near her. It was he who had been in the newspaper office when intelligence of the railroad disaster was received, with Brently Mallard's name leading the list of "killed."[37] He had only taken the time to assure himself of its truth by a second telegram, and had hastened to forestall any less careful, less tender friend in bearing the sad message.

She did not hear the story as many women have heard the same, with a paralyzed inability to accept its significance.[38] She wept at once, with sudden, wild abandonment, in her sister's arms. When the storm of grief had spent itself, she went away to her room alone. She would have no one follow her.[39]

There stood, facing the open window, a comfortable, roomy armchair.[40] Into this she sank, pressed down by a physical exhaustion that haunted her body and seemed to reach into her soul.[41]

She could see in the open square before her house the tops of trees that were all aquiver with the new spring life.[42] The delicious breath of rain was in the air. In the street below a peddler was crying his wares. The notes of a distant song which some one was singing reached her faintly, and countless sparrows were twittering in the eaves.[43]

There were patches of blue sky showing here and there through the clouds that had met and piled one above the other in the west facing her window.[44]

She sat with her head thrown back upon the cushion of the chair, quite motionless, except when a sob came up into her throat and shook her, as a child who has cried itself to sleep continues to sob in its dreams.

She was young, with a fair, calm face, whose lines bespoke repression and even a certain strength.[45] But now there was a dull stare in her eyes, whose gaze was fixed away off yonder on one of those patches of blue sky. It was not a glance of reflection, but rather indicated a suspension of intelligent thought.

There was something coming to her and she was waiting for it, fearfully. What was it? She did not know; it was too subtle and elusive to name. But she felt it, creeping out of the sky, reaching toward her through the sounds, the scents, the color that filled the air.[46]

Now her bosom rose and fell tumultuously. She was beginning to recognize this thing that was approaching to possess her, and she was striving to beat it back with her will—as powerless as her two white slender hands would have been. When she abandoned herself a little whispered word escaped her slightly parted lips. She said it over and over under the breath: "free, free, free!" The vacant stare and the look of terror that had followed it went from her eyes. They stayed keen and bright. Her pulses beat fast, and the coursing blood warmed and relaxed every inch of her body.[47]

She did not stop to ask if it were or were not a monstrous joy that held her.[48] A clear and exalted perception enabled her to dismiss the suggestion as trivial. She knew that she would weep again when she saw the kind, tender hands folded in death; the face that had never looked save with love upon her, fixed and gray and dead. But she saw beyond that bitter moment a long procession of years to come that would belong to her absolutely. And she opened and spread her arms out to them in welcome.

There would be no one to live for during those coming years; she would live for herself. There would be no powerful will bending hers in that blind persistence with which men and women believe they have a right to impose a private will upon a fellow-creature. A kind intention or a cruel intention made the act seem no less a crime as she looked upon it in that brief moment of illumination.

And yet she had loved him—sometimes. Often she had not. What did it matter! What could love, the unsolved mystery, count for in the face of this possession of self-assertion which she suddenly recognized as the strongest impulse of her being!

"Free! Body and soul free!" she kept whispering.

Josephine was kneeling before the closed door with her lips to the keyhole, imploring for admission. "Louise, open the door! I beg; open the door—you will make yourself ill. What are you doing, Louise? For heaven's sake open the door."

"Go away. I am not making myself ill." No; she was drinking in a very elixir of life through that open window.

Her fancy was running riot along those days ahead of her. Spring days, and summer days, and all sorts of days that would be her own. She breathed a quick prayer that life might be long. It was only yesterday she had thought with a shudder that life might be long.

She arose at length and opened the door to her sister's importunities. There was a feverish triumph in her eyes, and she carried herself unwittingly like a goddess of Victory. She clasped her sister's waist, and together they descended the stairs. Richards stood waiting for them at the bottom.

Someone was opening the front door with a latchkey. It was Brently Mallard who entered, a little travel-stained, composedly carrying his grip-sack and umbrella. He had been far from the scene of the accident, and did not even know there had been one. He stood amazed at Josephine's piercing cry; at Richards' quick motion to screen him from the view of his wife.

When the doctors came they said she had died of heart disease—of the joy that kills.[49]

DISCUSSION QUESTIONS

1. How does the author use names throughout the story? What is the significance of learning Louise Mallard's full name so late in the story? Why is she known as Mrs. Mallard for so much of it?

2. What is the importance of Louise Mallard's supposed "heart condition"? Do you think she actually has a heart condition, and if so, how is Chopin using this detail to develop themes within the story?

3. What is the characterization of Louise Mallard? What are some of the differences between the way in which other characters perceive her and the way in which she appears to the reader? Why does Chopin suggest a difference of perspective with regard to this character? Why is people's misjudgment of Louise so important?

4. What is the significance of the story's historical context? It is a contemporary story for Chopin, set during the time in which it was written. How does this impact your interpretation of characters and situations?

5. How does Louise Mallard appear to feel about her husband's death? How does Chopin represent the complexity of Louise Mallard's feelings? Why is this complexity important to the story? Why is it important that Louise Mallard isn't just happy or sad that her husband is dead?

6. What use does Chopin make of secondary characters within the story? Discuss the role of Louise's sister, Richards, and Mr. Mallard.

7. The narrator's remark at the end of the story is intensely ironic. Why does Chopin adopt this technique? How does it bring together the themes of the text and reinforce her main point so effectively?

VOCABULARY ACTIVITY

1. Locate each word in the text. Use context clues to create a definition for each word.

2. Use a dictionary and write a new definition in your own words that is more accurate.

- *Aquiver*
- *Bearing*
- *Bespoke*
- *Fancy*
- *Forestall*
- *Importunity*
- *Monstrous*
- *Sank*

SEMANTIC MAP

Instructions: You will create a semantic map of vocabulary words used in the story. Start by placing the assigned word in the middle of the page. Then add more information with lines that show the connections.

1. Use context clues and a dictionary to define the word.

2. Add synonyms and antonyms.

3. Include words or phrases that add to the meaning.

4. Add images that clarify the meaning. (Include image credits.)

5. Share your semantic map with other students and read theirs.

6. Use this page and the next to plan your poster-board.

CONNOTATION AND DENOTATION

Define Connotation

Define Denotation

1. Consider some of the different definitions for the word *blue*.

    a. The denotation of **blue**

    b. The connotation of **blue**

2. The story concludes with the observation that Mrs. Mallard dies from "the joy that kills." What are some different definitions of *joy*?

3. Provide an example from the text that supports the idea that *joy* may function ironically within the text.

4. Why do you think the author describes Mrs. Mallard as having died from *joy*? How do connotation and denotation change the meaning of the title?

5. Another set of words we should examine in "The Story of An Hour" are *free* and *repression*.

    What is the *denotation* of these two words?

    a. Free

    b. Repression

6. List a few examples of how the narrator uses these words in the text.

    a. Free

    b. Repression

7. Sometimes, the difference in the definition of words is partly due to the tone of the word, or the emotion we attach to it. For each word, is the tone *positive, negative, or neutral?*

    a. Free

    b. Repression

CHARACTER ANALYSIS

Authors combine the tools they use to create an engaging story. In this assignment, we will analyze the characters. However, it is important to remember that characters are a necessary part of the plot and contribute to the theme. Each of the author's tools, in this case, characterization, makes their other tools sharper. As you complete the analysis of these characters, consider what they have in common, what differs, and how their differences lead to their conflict.

Character Name: Louise Mallard

1. Appearance
   a. Answer in your own words
   b. Provide a quotation to support your answer

2. Background information
   a. Answer in your own words
   b. Provide a quotation to support your answer

3. Interests and values
   a. Answer in your own words
   b. Provide a quotation to support your answer

4. How does she feel about her husband's death?
   a. Answer in your own words
   b. Provide a quotation to support your answer

5. How do her values impact the way she approaches life?
   a. Answer in your own words
   b. Provide a quotation to support your answer

THEME ANALYSIS

Theme is a core statement of an author's message in their writing. Stories may have more than one theme deliberately included by the author, and they may generate ideas about unintended themes in the reader.

When we talk about theme in literature, sometimes we talk about a single word or short phrase that identifies the core idea in the theme. For example, If you were discussing *Romeo and Juliet*, you might say the theme is "love." When moving to writing about theme, though, we need to add more context to the idea than just one word. A strong analysis of the theme will lead to a theme statement.

1. List 3 theme words or short phrases from "The Story of An Hour."

2. Next, we want to create a complete sentence about the theme. Remember that the theme statement will not include specific details from the story. Use the theme "the value of human life" to create a theme statement.

    a. What does the author, Kate Chopin, want the readers to think about the circumstances of Louise Mallard's life?

    b. Write your final theme statement here

WRITING ASSIGNMENT

Instructions: Using your notes on character, theme, setting, and context, as well as the annotated text provided, write an essay that addresses the following prompt.

How does the characterization of Louise Mallard contribute to the theme of "The Story of An Hour"?

The Garden Party

by Katherine Mansfield (1922)

AND after all the weather was ideal.[50] They could not have had a more perfect day for a garden-party if they had ordered it. Windless, warm, the sky without a cloud. Only the blue was veiled with a haze of light gold, as it is sometimes in early summer. The gardener had been up since dawn, mowing the lawns and sweeping them, until the grass and the dark flat rosettes where the daisy plants had been seemed to shine.[51] As for the roses, you could not help feeling they understood that roses are the only flowers that impress people at garden-parties; the only flowers that everybody is certain of knowing. Hundreds, yes, literally hundreds, had come out in a single night; the green bushes bowed down as though they had been visited by archangels.

Breakfast was not yet over before the men came to put up the marquee.

"Where do you want the marquee put, mother?"[52]

"My dear child, it's no use asking me. I'm determined to leave everything to you children this year. Forget I am your mother. Treat me as an honoured guest."[53]

But Meg could not possibly go and supervise the men. She had washed her hair before breakfast, and she sat drinking her coffee in a green turban, with a dark wet curl stamped on each cheek. Jose, the butterfly, always came down in a silk petticoat and a kimono jacket.

"You'll have to go, Laura; you're the artistic one."

Away Laura flew, still holding her piece of bread-and-butter. It's so delicious to have an excuse for eating out of doors, and besides, she loved having to arrange things; she always felt she could do it so much better than anybody else.

Four men in their shirt-sleeves stood grouped together on the garden path. They carried staves covered with rolls of canvas, and they had big tool-bags slung on their backs. They looked impressive. Laura wished now that she had not got the bread-and-butter, but there was nowhere to put it, and she couldn't possibly throw it away. She blushed and tried to look severe and even a little bit short-sighted as she came up to them.

"Good morning," she said, copying her mother's voice. But that sounded so fearfully affected that she was ashamed, and stammered like a little girl, "Oh—er—have you come—is it about the marquee?"

"That's right, miss," said the tallest of the men, a lanky, freckled fellow, and he shifted his tool-bag, knocked back his straw hat and smiled down at her. "That's about it."

His smile was so easy, so friendly that Laura recovered. What nice eyes he had, small, but such a dark blue! And now she looked at the others, they were smiling too. "Cheer up, we won't bite," their smile seemed to say. How very nice workmen were! And what a beautiful morning! She mustn't mention the morning; she must be business-like. The marquee.

"Well, what about the lily-lawn? Would that do?"

And she pointed to the lily-lawn with the hand that didn't hold the bread-and-butter. They turned, they stared in the direction. A little fat chap thrust out his under-lip, and the tall fellow frowned.

"I don't fancy it," said he. "Not conspicuous enough. You see, with a thing like a marquee," and he turned to Laura in his easy way, "you want to put it somewhere where it'll give you a bang slap in the eye, if you follow me."

Laura's upbringing made her wonder for a moment whether it was quite respectful of a workman to talk to her of bangs slap in the eye.[54] But she did quite follow him.

"A corner of the tennis-court," she suggested. "But the band's going to be in one corner."

"H'm, going to have a band, are you?" said another of the workmen. He was pale. He had a haggard look as his dark eyes scanned the tennis-court. What was he thinking?

"Only a very small band," said Laura gently. Perhaps he wouldn't mind so much if the band was quite small. But the tall fellow interrupted.

"Look here, miss, that's the place. Against those trees. Over there. That'll do fine."

Against the karakas. Then the karaka-trees would be hidden. And they were so lovely, with their broad, gleaming leaves, and their clusters of yellow fruit. They were like trees you imagined growing on a desert island, proud, solitary, lifting their leaves and fruits to the sun in a kind of silent splendour. Must they be hidden by a marquee?[55]

They must. Already the men had shouldered their staves and were making for the place. Only the tall fellow was left. He bent down, pinched a sprig of lavender, put his thumb and forefinger to his nose and snuffed up the smell. When Laura saw that gesture she forgot all about the karakas in her wonder at him caring for things like that—caring for the smell of lavender. How many men that she knew would have done such a thing? Oh, how extraordinarily nice workmen were, she thought. Why couldn't she have workmen for her friends rather than the silly boys she danced with and who came to Sunday night supper?[56] She would get on much better with men like these.

It's all the fault, she decided, as the tall fellow drew something on the back of an envelope, something that was to be looped up or left to hang, of these absurd class distinctions. Well, for her part, she didn't feel them. Not a bit, not an atom … And now there came the chock-chock of wooden hammers. Some one whistled, some one sang out, "Are you right there, matey?" "Matey!" The friendliness of it, the—the— Just to prove how happy she was, just to show the tall fellow how at home she felt, and how she despised stupid conventions, Laura took a big bite of her bread-and-butter as she stared at the little drawing. She felt just like a work-girl.

"Laura, Laura, where are you? Telephone, Laura!" a voice cried from the house.

"Coming!" Away she skimmed, over the lawn, up the path, up the steps, across the veranda, and into the porch. In the hall her father and Laurie were brushing their hats ready to go to the office.

"I say, Laura," said Laurie very fast, "you might just give a squiz at my coat before this afternoon. See if it wants pressing."

"I will," said she. Suddenly she couldn't stop herself. She ran at Laurie and gave him a small, quick squeeze. "Oh, I do love parties, don't you?" gasped Laura.

"Ra-ther," said Laurie's warm, boyish voice, and he squeezed his sister too, and gave her a gentle push. "Dash off to the telephone, old girl."

The telephone. "Yes, yes; oh yes. Kitty? Good morning, dear. Come to lunch? Do, dear. Delighted of course. It will only be a very scratch meal—just the sandwich crusts and broken meringue-shells and what's left over. Yes, isn't it a perfect morning? Your white? Oh, I certainly should. One moment—hold the line. Mother's calling." And Laura sat back. "What, mother? Can't hear."

Mrs. Sheridan's voice floated down the stairs. "Tell her to wear that sweet hat she had on last Sunday."

"Mother says you're to wear that sweet hat you had on last Sunday. Good. One o'clock. Bye-bye."

Laura put back the receiver, flung her arms over her head, took a deep breath, stretched and let them fall. "Huh," she sighed, and the moment after the sigh she sat up quickly. She was still, listening. All the doors in the house seemed to be open. The house was alive with soft, quick steps and running voices. The green baize door that led to the kitchen regions swung open and shut with a muffled thud. And now there came a long, chuckling absurd sound. It was the heavy piano being moved on its stiff castors. But the air! If you stopped to notice, was the air always like this? Little faint winds were playing chase, in at the tops of the windows, out at the doors. And there were two tiny spots of sun, one on the inkpot, one on a silver photograph frame, playing too. Darling little spots. Especially the one on the inkpot lid. It was quite warm. A warm little silver star. She could have kissed it.

The front door bell pealed, and there sounded the rustle of Sadie's print skirt on the stairs. A man's voice murmured; Sadie answered, careless, "I'm sure I don't know. Wait. I'll ask Mrs Sheridan."

"What is it, Sadie?" Laura came into the hall.

"It's the florist, Miss Laura."

It was, indeed. There, just inside the door, stood a wide, shallow tray full of pots of pink lilies. No other kind. Nothing but lilies—canna lilies, big pink flowers, wide open, radiant, almost frighteningly alive on bright crimson stems.

"O-oh, Sadie!" said Laura, and the sound was like a little moan. She crouched down as if to warm herself at that blaze of lilies; she felt they were in her fingers, on her lips, growing in her breast.

"It's some mistake," she said faintly. "Nobody ever ordered so many. Sadie, go and find mother."

But at that moment Mrs. Sheridan joined them.

"It's quite right," she said calmly. "Yes, I ordered them. Aren't they lovely?" She pressed Laura's arm. "I was passing the shop yesterday, and I saw them in the window. And I suddenly thought for once in my life I shall have enough canna lilies. The garden-party will be a good excuse."[57]

"But I thought you said you didn't mean to interfere," said Laura. Sadie had gone. The florist's man was still outside at his van. She put her arm round her mother's neck and gently, very gently, she bit her mother's ear.

"My darling child, you wouldn't like a logical mother, would you? Don't do that. Here's the man."

He carried more lilies still, another whole tray.

"Bank them up, just inside the door, on both sides of the porch, please," said Mrs. Sheridan. "Don't you agree, Laura?"

"Oh, I do, mother."

In the drawing-room Meg, Jose and good little Hans had at last succeeded in moving the piano.

"Now, if we put this chesterfield against the wall and move everything out of the room except the chairs, don't you think?"

"Quite."

"Hans, move these tables into the smoking-room, and bring a sweeper to take these marks off the carpet and—one moment, Hans—" Jose loved giving orders to the servants, and they loved obeying her. She always made them feel they were taking part in some drama. "Tell mother and Miss Laura to come here at once."

"Very good, Miss Jose."

She turned to Meg. "I want to hear what the piano sounds like, just in case I'm asked to sing this afternoon. Let's try over 'This life is Weary.'"

Pom! Ta-ta-ta Tee-ta! The piano burst out so passionately that Jose's face changed. She clasped her hands. She looked mournfully and enigmatically at her mother and Laura as they came in.

"This Life is Wee-ary, A Tear—a Sigh. A Love that Chan-ges, This Life is Wee-ary, A Tear—a Sigh. A Love that Chan-ges, And then ... Good-bye!"

But at the word "Good-bye," and although the piano sounded more desperate than ever, her face broke into a brilliant, dreadfully unsympathetic smile.

"Aren't I in good voice, mummy?" she beamed.

"This Life is Wee-ary, Hope comes to Die. A Dream—a Wa-kening."

But now Sadie interrupted them. "What is it, Sadie?"

"If you please, m'm, cook says have you got the flags for the sandwiches?"

"The flags for the sandwiches, Sadie?" echoed Mrs. Sheridan dreamily. And the children knew by her face that she hadn't got them. "Let me see." And she said to Sadie firmly, "Tell cook I'll let her have them in ten minutes."

Sadie went.

"Now, Laura," said her mother quickly, "come with me into the smoking-room. I've got the names somewhere on the back of an envelope. You'll have to write them out for me. Meg, go upstairs this minute and take that wet thing off your head. Jose, run and finish dressing this instant. Do you hear me, children, or shall I have to tell your father when he comes home to-night? And—and, Jose, pacify cook if you do go into the kitchen, will you? I'm terrified of her this morning."

The envelope was found at last behind the dining-room clock, though how it had got there Mrs. Sheridan could not imagine.

"One of you children must have stolen it out of my bag, because I remember vividly—cream cheese and lemon-curd. Have you done that?"

"Yes."

"Egg and—"Mrs. Sheridan held the envelope away from her. "It looks like mice. It can't be mice, can it?"

"Olive, pet," said Laura, looking over her shoulder.

"Yes, of course, olive. What a horrible combination it sounds. Egg and olive."

They were finished at last, and Laura took them off to the kitchen. She found Jose there pacifying the cook, who did not look at all terrifying.

"I have never seen such exquisite sandwiches," said Jose's rapturous voice. "How many kinds did you say there were, cook? Fifteen?"

"Fifteen, Miss Jose."

"Well, cook, I congratulate you."

Cook swept up crusts with the long sandwich knife, and smiled broadly.

"Godber's has come," announced Sadie, issuing out of the pantry. She had seen the man pass the window.

That meant the cream puffs had come. Godber's were famous for their cream puffs. Nobody ever thought of making them at home.

"Bring them in and put them on the table, my girl," ordered cook.

Sadie brought them in and went back to the door. Of course Laura and Jose were far too grown-up to really care about such things. All the same, they couldn't help agreeing that the puffs looked very attractive. Very. Cook began arranging them, shaking off the extra icing sugar.

"Don't they carry one back to all one's parties?" said Laura.

"I suppose they do," said practical Jose, who never liked to be carried back. "They look beautifully light and feathery, I must say."

"Have one each, my dears," said cook in her comfortable voice. "Yer ma won't know."

Oh, impossible. Fancy cream puffs so soon after breakfast. The very idea made one shudder. All the same, two minutes later Jose and Laura were licking their fingers with that absorbed inward look that only comes from whipped cream.

"Let's go into the garden, out by the back way," suggested Laura. "I want to see how the men are getting on with the marquee. They're such awfully nice men."

But the back door was blocked by cook, Sadie, Godber's man and Hans.

Something had happened.

"Tuk-tuk-tuk," clucked cook like an agitated hen. Sadie had her hand clapped to her cheek as though she had toothache. Hans's face was screwed up in the effort to understand. Only Godber's man seemed to be enjoying himself; it was his story.

"What's the matter? What's happened?"

"There's been a horrible accident," said Cook. "A man killed."

"A man killed! Where? How? When?"[58]

But Godber's man wasn't going to have his story snatched from under his very nose.

"Know those little cottages just below here, miss?" Know them? Of course, she knew them. "Well, there's a young chap living there, name of Scott, a carter. His horse shied at a traction-engine, corner of Hawke Street this morning, and he was thrown out on the back of his head. Killed."

"Dead!" Laura stared at Godber's man.

"Dead when they picked him up," said Godber's man with relish. "They were taking the body home as I come up here." And he said to the cook, "He's left a wife and five little ones."

"Jose, come here." Laura caught hold of her sister's sleeve and dragged her through the kitchen to the other side of the green baize door. There she paused and leaned against it. "Jose!" she said, horrified, "however are we going to stop everything?"[59]

"Stop everything, Laura!" cried Jose in astonishment. "What do you mean?"

"Stop the garden-party, of course." Why did Jose pretend?

But Jose was still more amazed. "Stop the garden-party? My dear Laura, don't be so absurd. Of course we can't do anything of the kind. Nobody expects us to. Don't be so extravagant."[60]

"But we can't possibly have a garden-party with a man dead just outside the front gate."[61]

That really was extravagant, for the little cottages were in a lane to themselves at the very bottom of a steep rise that led up to the house. A broad road ran between. True, they were far too near. They were the greatest possible eyesore, and they had no right to be in that neighbourhood at all. They were little mean dwellings painted a chocolate brown. In the garden patches there was nothing but cabbage stalks, sick hens and tomato cans. The very smoke coming out of their chimneys was poverty-stricken. Little rags and shreds of smoke, so unlike the great silvery plumes that uncurled from the Sheridans' chimneys. Washerwomen lived in the lane and sweeps and a cobbler, and a man whose house-front was studded all over with minute bird-cages. Children swarmed. When the Sheridans were little they were forbidden to set foot there because of the revolting language and of what they might catch. But since they were grown up, Laura and Laurie on their prowls sometimes walked through. It was disgusting and sordid. They came out with a shudder.

But still one must go everywhere; one must see everything. So through they went.[62]

"And just think of what the band would sound like to that poor woman," said Laura.

"Oh, Laura!" Jose began to be seriously annoyed. "If you're going to stop a band playing every time some one has an accident, you'll lead a very strenuous life. I'm every bit as sorry about it as you. I feel just as sympathetic." Her eyes hardened. She looked at her sister just as she used to when they were little and fighting together. "You won't bring a drunken workman back to life by being sentimental," she said softly.

"Drunk! Who said he was drunk?" Laura turned furiously on Jose. She said, just as they had used to say on those occasions, "I'm going straight up to tell mother."[63]

"Do, dear," cooed Jose.

"Mother, can I come into your room?" Laura turned the big glass door-knob.

"Of course, child. Why, what's the matter? What's given you such a colour?" And Mrs. Sheridan turned round from her dressing-table. She was trying on a new hat.

"Mother, a man's been killed," began Laura.

"Not in the garden?" interrupted her mother.

"No, no!"

"Oh, what a fright you gave me!" Mrs. Sheridan sighed with relief, and took off the big hat and held it on her knees.

"But listen, mother," said Laura. Breathless, half-choking, she told the dreadful story. "Of course, we can't have our party, can we?" she pleaded. "The band and everybody arriving. They'd hear us, mother; they're nearly neighbours!"

To Laura's astonishment her mother behaved just like Jose; it was harder to bear because she seemed amused. She refused to take Laura seriously.[64]

"But, my dear child, use your common sense. It's only by accident we've heard of it. If some one had died there normally—and I can't understand how they keep alive in those poky little holes—we should still be having our party, shouldn't we?"

Laura had to say "yes" to that, but she felt it was all wrong. She sat down on her mother's sofa and pinched the cushion frill.

"Mother, isn't it terribly heartless of us?" she asked.

"Darling!" Mrs. Sheridan got up and came over to her, carrying the hat. Before Laura could stop her she had popped it on. "My child!" said her mother, "the hat is yours. It's made for you. It's much too young for me. I have never seen you look such a picture. Look at yourself!" And she held up her hand-mirror.[65]

"But, mother," Laura began again. She couldn't look at herself; she turned aside.

This time Mrs. Sheridan lost patience just as Jose had done.

"You are being very absurd, Laura," she said coldly. "People like that don't expect sacrifices from us. And it's not very sympathetic to spoil everybody's enjoyment as you're doing now."[66]

"I don't understand," said Laura, and she walked quickly out of the room into her own bedroom. There, quite by chance, the first thing she saw was this charming girl in the mirror, in her black hat trimmed with gold daisies, and a long black velvet ribbon. Never had she imagined she could look like that.[67] Is mother right? she thought. And now she hoped her mother was right. Am I being extravagant? Perhaps it was extravagant. Just for a moment she had another glimpse of that poor woman and those little children, and the body being carried into the house. But it all seemed blurred, unreal, like a picture in the newspaper. I'll remember it again after the party's over, she decided. And somehow that seemed quite the best plan …

Lunch was over by half-past one. By half-past two they were all ready for the fray. The green-coated band had arrived and was established in a corner of the tennis-court.

"My dear!" trilled Kitty Maitland, "aren't they too like frogs for words? You ought to have arranged them round the pond with the conductor in the middle on a leaf."

Laurie arrived and hailed them on his way to dress. At the sight of him Laura remembered the accident again. She wanted to tell him. If Laurie agreed with the others, then it was bound to be all right. And she followed him into the hall.

"Laurie!"

"Hallo!" He was half-way upstairs, but when he turned round and saw Laura he suddenly puffed out his cheeks and goggled his eyes at her. "My word, Laura! You do look stunning," said Laurie. "What an absolutely topping hat!"

Laura said faintly "Is it?" and smiled up at Laurie, and didn't tell him after all.

Soon after that people began coming in streams. The band struck up; the hired waiters ran from the house to the marquee. Wherever you looked there were couples strolling, bending to the flowers, greeting, moving on over the lawn. They were like bright birds that had alighted in the Sheridans' garden for this one afternoon, on their way to—where? Ah, what happiness it is to be with people who all are happy, to press hands, press cheeks, smile into eyes.

"Darling Laura, how well you look!"

"What a becoming hat, child!"

"Laura, you look quite Spanish. I've never seen you look so striking."

And Laura, glowing, answered softly, "Have you had tea? Won't you have an ice? The passion-fruit ices really are rather special." She ran to her father and begged him. "Daddy darling, can't the band have something to drink?"

And the perfect afternoon slowly ripened, slowly faded, slowly its petals closed.

"Never a more delightful garden-party ..." "The greatest success ..." "Quite the most ..."

Laura helped her mother with the good-byes. They stood side by side in the porch till it was all over.

"All over, all over, thank heaven," said Mrs. Sheridan. "Round up the others, Laura. Let's go and have some fresh coffee. I'm exhausted. Yes, it's been very successful. But oh, these parties, these parties! Why will you children insist on giving parties!"[68] And they all of them sat down in the deserted marquee.

"Have a sandwich, daddy dear. I wrote the flag."

"Thanks." Mr. Sheridan took a bite and the sandwich was gone. He took another. "I suppose you didn't hear of a beastly accident that happened to-day?" he said.

"My dear," said Mrs. Sheridan, holding up her hand, "we did. It nearly ruined the party. Laura insisted we should put it off."

"Oh, mother!" Laura didn't want to be teased about it.

"It was a horrible affair all the same," said Mr. Sheridan. "The chap was married too. Lived just below in the lane, and leaves a wife and half a dozen kiddies, so they say."[69]

An awkward little silence fell. Mrs. Sheridan fidgeted with her cup. Really, it was very tactless of father ...

Suddenly she looked up. There on the table were all those sandwiches, cakes, puffs, all uneaten, all going to be wasted. She had one of her brilliant ideas.

"I know," she said. "Let's make up a basket. Let's send that poor creature some of this perfectly good food. At any rate, it will be the greatest treat for the children. Don't you agree? And she's sure to have neighbours calling in and so on. What a point to have it all ready prepared. Laura!" She jumped up. "Get me the big basket out of the stairs cupboard."

"But, mother, do you really think it's a good idea?" said Laura.

Again, how curious, she seemed to be different from them all. To take scraps from their party. Would the poor woman really like that?

"Of course! What's the matter with you to-day? An hour or two ago you were insisting on us being sympathetic, and now—"[70]

Oh well! Laura ran for the basket. It was filled, it was heaped by her mother.

"Take it yourself, darling," said she. "Run down just as you are. No, wait, take the arum lilies too. People of that class are so impressed by arum lilies."[71]

"The stems will ruin her lace frock," said practical Jose.

So they would. Just in time. "Only the basket, then. And, Laura!"—her mother followed her out of the marquee— "don't on any account—"

"What mother?"

No, better not put such ideas into the child's head! "Nothing! Run along."

It was just growing dusky as Laura shut their garden gates. A big dog ran by like a shadow. The road gleamed white, and down below in the hollow the little cottages were in deep shade. How quiet it seemed after the afternoon. Here she was going down the hill to somewhere where a man lay dead, and she couldn't realize it. Why couldn't she? She stopped a minute. And it seemed to her that kisses, voices, tinkling spoons, laughter, the smell of crushed grass were somehow inside her. She had no room for anything else. How strange! She looked up at the pale sky, and all she thought was, "Yes, it was the most successful party."

Now the broad road was crossed. The lane began, smoky and dark. Women in shawls and men's tweed caps hurried by. Men hung over the palings; the children played in the doorways. A low hum came from the mean little cottages.

In some of them there was a flicker of light, and a shadow, crab-like, moved across the window. Laura bent her head and hurried on. She wished now she had put on a coat. How her frock shone! And the big hat with the velvet streamer— if only it was another hat! Were the people looking at her? They must be. It was a mistake to have come; she knew all along it was a mistake. Should she go back even now?

No, too late. This was the house. It must be. A dark knot of people stood outside. Beside the gate an old, old woman with a crutch sat in a chair, watching. She had her feet on a newspaper. The voices stopped as Laura drew near. The group parted. It was as though she was expected, as though they had known she was coming here.

Laura was terribly nervous. Tossing the velvet ribbon over her shoulder, she said to a woman standing by, "Is this Mrs. Scott's house?" and the woman, smiling queerly, said, "It is, my lass."

Oh, to be away from this! She actually said, "Help me, God," as she walked up the tiny path and knocked. To be away from those staring eyes, or to be covered up in anything, one of those women's shawls even. I'll just leave the basket and go, she decided. I shan't even wait for it to be emptied.

Then the door opened. A little woman in black showed in the gloom.

Laura said, "Are you Mrs. Scott?" But to her horror the woman answered, "Walk in please, miss," and she was shut in the passage.

"No," said Laura, "I don't want to come in. I only want to leave this basket. Mother sent—"

The little woman in the gloomy passage seemed not to have heard her. "Step this way, please, miss," she said in an oily voice, and Laura followed her.

She found herself in a wretched little low kitchen, lighted by a smoky lamp. There was a woman sitting before the fire.

"Em," said the little creature who had let her in. "Em! It's a young lady." She turned to Laura. She said meaningly, "I'm 'er sister, miss. You'll excuse 'er, won't you?"

"Oh, but of course!" said Laura. "Please, please don't disturb her. I—I only want to leave—"

But at that moment the woman at the fire turned round. Her face, puffed up, red, with swollen eyes and swollen lips, looked terrible. She seemed as though she couldn't understand why Laura was there. What did it mean? Why was this stranger standing in the kitchen with a basket? What was it all about? And the poor face puckered up again.

"All right, my dear," said the other. "I'll thenk the young lady."

And again she began, "You'll excuse her, miss, I'm sure," and her face, swollen too, tried an oily smile.

Laura only wanted to get out, to get away. She was back in the passage. The door opened. She walked straight through into the bedroom, where the dead man was lying.

"You'd like a look at 'im, wouldn't you?" said Em's sister, and she brushed past Laura over to the bed. "Don't be afraid, my lass,"—and now her voice sounded fond and sly, and fondly she drew down the sheet—" e looks a picture. There's nothing to show. Come along, my dear."

Laura came.

There lay a young man, fast asleep—sleeping so soundly, so deeply, that he was far, far away from them both. Oh, so remote, so peaceful. He was dreaming. Never wake him up again. His head was sunk in the pillow, his eyes were closed; they were blind under the closed eyelids. He was given up to his dream. What did garden-parties and baskets and lace frocks matter to him? He was far from all those things. He was wonderful, beautiful. While they were laughing and while the band was playing, this marvel had come to the lane. Happy … happy … All is well, said that sleeping face. This is just as it should be. I am content.[72]

But all the same you had to cry, and she couldn't go out of the room without saying something to him. Laura gave a loud childish sob.

"Forgive my hat," she said.

And this time she didn't wait for Em's sister. She found her way out of the door, down the path, past all those dark people. At the corner of the lane she met Laurie.

He stepped out of the shadow. "Is that you, Laura?"

"Yes."

"Mother was getting anxious. Was it all right?"

"Yes, quite. Oh, Laurie!" She took his arm, she pressed up against him.

"I say, you're not crying, are you?" asked her brother.

Laura shook her head. She was.

Laurie put his arm round her shoulder. "Don't cry," he said in his warm, loving voice. "Was it awful?"

"No," sobbed Laura. "It was simply marvellous. But Laurie—" She stopped, she looked at her brother. "Isn't life," she stammered, "isn't life—" But what life was she couldn't explain. No matter. He quite understood.[73]

"Isn't it, darling?" said Laurie.

DISCUSSION QUESTIONS

1. When and where does the story take place, and how does Mansfield establish this context?

2. Who are the Sheridans and what kind of life do they lead based on the information within the story?

3. What is the narrative perspective of the story? What kind of narrator does Mansfield use and why? How does this narrative perspective affect the reader's response to the story?

4. Who is "Godber's man" and what is his significance to the story? How do his behavior and reaction contrast with that of Laura and Jose? What is the significance of this difference?

5. Why does Mrs. Sheridan proceed with the party? What arguments does she offer to justify her decision?

6. What do Mrs. Sheridan's hat and hand mirror symbolize?

7. What is the significance of the garden party in the end? Why does Mansfield not conclude the story with the party? What is the eventual tone of the party?

8. What is the significance of the Scotts' lower-class status? How does Mansfield convey their status to the reader? Why are the Sheridans so class-conscious? Is Laura as class-conscious as her mother, and why?

VOCABULARY ACTIVITY

1. Locate each word in the text. Use context clues to create a definition for each word.

2. Use a dictionary and write a new definition in your own words that is more accurate.

- *Absurd*
- *Beastly*
- *Conspicuous*
- *Extravagant*
- *Haggard*
- *Lanky*
- *Plume*
- *Queerly*
- *Rapturous*
- *Shied*
- *Sordid*

SEMANTIC MAP

Instructions: You will create a semantic map of vocabulary words used in the story. Start by placing the assigned word in the middle of the page. Then add more information with lines that show the connections.

1. Use context clues and a dictionary to define the word.

2. Add synonyms and antonyms.

3. Include words or phrases that add to the meaning.

4. Add images that clarify the meaning. (Include image credits.)

5. Share your semantic map with other students and read theirs.

6. Use this page and the next to plan your poster-board.

CONNOTATION AND DENOTATION

Define Connotation

Define Denotation

1. Consider some of the different definitions for the word *party*.
    a. The denotation of **party**
    b. The connotation of **party**

2. The story concludes with Laura declaring that what she sees of life is "marvellous." What are some different definitions of *marvelous*?

3. Provide an example from the text that supports the idea that *marvelous* may have several different meanings within the text.

4. Why do you think the author has Laura declare that what she experiences of life, seeing the dead man, is *marvelous*? How do connotation and denotation change the message of the story through this observation?

5. Another set of words we should examine in "The Garden Party" are *sympathetic* and *appropriate*.
    What is the *denotation* of these two words?

6. List a few examples of how the characters use these words in the text.
    a. Sympathetic
    b. Appropriate

7. Sometimes, the difference in the definition of words is partly due to the tone of the word, or the emotion we attach to it. For each word, is the tone *positive*, *negative*, or *neutral?*

   a. Sympathetic

   b. Appropriate

CHARACTER ANALYSIS

Authors combine the tools they use to create an engaging story. In this assignment, we will analyze the characters. However, it is important to remember that characters are a necessary part of the plot and contribute to the theme. Each of the author's tools, in this case, characterization, makes their other tools sharper. As you complete the analysis of these characters, consider what they have in common, what differs, and how their differences lead to their conflict.

Character Name: Laura Sheridan

1. Appearance
   a. Answer in your own words
   b. Provide a quotation to support your answer

2. Background information
   a. Answer in your own words
   b. Provide a quotation to support your answer

3. Interests and values
   a. Answer in your own words
   b. Provide a quotation to support your answer

4. How does she feel about the garden party and the neighbor's death?
   a. Answer in your own words
   b. Provide a quotation to support your answer

5. How do her values impact the way she approaches life?
   a. Answer in your own words
   b. Provide a quotation to support your answer

Character Name: Laurie Sheridan

1. Appearance
   a. Answer in your own words
   b. Provide a quotation to support your answer

2. Background information
   a. Answer in your own words
   b. Provide a quotation to support your answer

3. Interests and values
   a. Answer in your own words
   b. Provide a quotation to support your answer

4. How does he feel about the garden party and the neighbor's death?
   a. Answer in your own words
   b. Provide a quotation to support your answer

5. How do his values impact the way he approaches life?
   a. Answer in your own words
   b. Provide a quotation to support your answer

Character Name: Mrs. Sheridan

1. Appearance
   a. Answer in your own words
   b. Provide a quotatio to support your answer

2. Background information
   a. Answer in your own words
   b. Provide a quotation to support your answer

3. Interests and values

    a. Answer in your own words

    b. Provide a quotation to support your answer

4. How does she feel about the garden party and the neighbor's death?

    a. Answer in your own words

    b. Provide a quotation to support your answer

5. How do her values impact the way she approaches life?

    a. Answer in your own words

    b. Provide a quotation to support your answer

THEME ANALYSIS

Theme is a core statement of an author's message in their writing. Stories may have more than one theme deliberately included by the author, and they may generate ideas about unintended themes in the reader.

When we talk about theme in literature, sometimes we talk about a single word or short phrase that identifies the core idea in the theme. For example, If you were discussing *Romeo and Juliet*, you might say the theme is "love." When moving to writing about theme, though, we need to add more context to the idea than just one word. A strong analysis of the theme will lead to a theme statement.

1. List 3 theme words or short phrases from "The Garden Party."

2. Next, we want to create a complete sentence about the theme. Remember that the theme statement will not include specific details from the story. Use the theme "the value of human life" to create a theme statement.

   a. What does the author, Katherine Mansfield, want the readers to think about the tension between the garden party and neighbor's death?

   b. Write your final theme statement here

WRITING ASSIGNMENT

Instructions: Using your notes on character, theme, setting, and context, as well as the annotated text provided, write an essay that addresses the following prompt:

How does Katherine Mansfield's representation of class difference and class bias in "The Garden Party" complicate the behavior of the Sheridan family, including Laura, when they hear news about the dead man?

SECTION TWO
Text Insights

The Most Dangerous Game

by Richard Connell (1924)

HISTORICAL AND THEMATIC CONTEXT

"**THE** Most Dangerous Game" is a short story written by American author and journalist Richard Connell in 1924. Originally called "The Hounds of Zaroff," and published in *Collier's*, a popular magazine, the story has often been adapted into radio plays, television series, and films. It is considered one of the most popular and influential short stories ever written.

Given its publication date and Rainsford's own recollection of fighting, the story has obvious associations with World War I (1914-1918), in addition to the Russian Revolution, which Connell references directly through General Zaroff. World War I was known as "the Great War" or "the War to End All Wars" because of the extent of the violence and the catastrophic loss of life. Many criticized how the war was fought, suggesting that those in power (usually those from the upper classes) showed a callous disregard for human life and were otherwise incompetent. Since Rainsford recalls the horrors of war as he is being hunted, Connell clarifies the connection between warfare and hunting, especially the "two classes" idea that facilitates the latter.

The Russian Revolution, which began in 1917 with the overthrow of Tsar Nicholas II, was also a major event in world history that saw large numbers of people killed, horrendous violence, and disruption to class systems. There were stories from the Revolution that suggest that some people were abusing their power of command. By having two Russian characters in the story—General Zaroff and Ivan—Connell draws a clear connection to the Revolution and its violence especially.

Finally, the allusions to big-game hunting draw on a tradition established by Europeans (and some Americans) of traveling to so-called exotic locations like Africa, Asia, or South America solely to hunt for amusement. Drawing a comparison between hunting traditions and war, Connell alludes to the role of imperialism in promoting violence, and he suggests that the practice of big-game hunting, much like war, is a kind of exploitation.

CHARACTER INSIGHTS

Sanger Rainsford is a big-game hunter with an international reputation. He is traveling to the Amazon with his friend Whitney when he hears distant gunshots and accidentally falls overboard. Although he initially articulates the worldview that the story challenges when he becomes the prey, hunted by Zaroff, his reflections about his experiences of war and hunting transform his perspective. He ultimately outwits Zaroff by drawing on his experiences as a soldier and a hunter, and by shifting his world-view to accommodate the idea that he is nothing more than an animal to Zaroff.

General Zaroff is a Russian Cossack, living on an island known as Ship-Trap, apparently in exile from post-Revolutionary Russia. He is a striking but savage figure, who takes a sadistic pleasure in hunting men and killing them. Although he claims to be both a gentleman and a sportsman, his callous disregard for human life cast doubt on his values from the first. Seeing Rainsford as the ultimate prey, the thrill he gets from hunting emphasizes the brutality of his behavior and contrasts sharply with the fear that Rainsford admits to when he himself is hunted.

Ivan is General Zaroff's deaf and mute assistant. He is incredibly tall and strong. He is also a Cossack. Employed to torture and kill the men that Zaroff hunts, Ivan's deafness and his inability to speak are important because they suggest his lack of attention to the suffering of others. He is literally deaf and mute, yes, but he is also metaphorically so, since he does nothing to protect people from the General.

Whitney is Rainsford's companion and friend. He initially points out Ship-Trap island and alludes to the stories told about it by sailors.

VOCABULARY RESOURCE

Amenities—*noun*; features of a facility that make it comfortable and pleasant

Elude—*verb*; to avoid or escape from someone or something by using cleverness

Feudal—*adjective*; relating to the feudal system of government, which was used primarily in Middle Ages Europe; the feudal system was based on land ownership and management, with the king at the top of the political structure and peasants or serfs at the bottom.

Futile—*adjective*; useless or ineffective

Indolent—*adjective*; avoiding work, being lazy or inactive

Opaque—*adjective*; not transparent; light cannot pass through it

Palpable—*adjective*; 1. plainly apparent; obvious, 2. something that can be touched or felt

Repast—*noun*; a meal

Scruples—*noun*; a set of morals that define a person's behavior

Staccato—*adjective*; sharp disconnected sounds

Tangible—*adjective*; able to be touched or felt

Vitality—*noun*; ability to survive; physical and mental strength

SAMPLE ESSAY

"The Most Dangerous Game" (1924) by Richard Connell is a popular short story exploring the difference between human and animal behavior. The central protagonist, Sanger Rainsford, is a famous hunter. Traveling to the Amazon rainforest with a friend, Rainsford falls overboard after hearing gunshots at a distance. He swims to what is known as Ship-Trap Island, a place that sailors describe as evil. Exploring the island, Rainsford encounters General Zaroff and his servant, Ivan, both of whom are Cossacks and fugitives of the Russian Revolution. Excited to have Rainsford on the island, General Zaroff explains that he purchased it and designed it to indulge his love of hunting. Instead of animals, though, General Zaroff hunts humans—men he lures to the island, imprisons, and "trains" to make them worthy adversaries. To Rainsford, he complains about the lack of competition; he justifies murder by applying a warped conception of Darwinism, arguing that "life is for the strong." General Zaroff's behavior ultimately challenges Rainsford's own worldview that there are "two classes—the hunters and the huntees," forcing him to reevaluate this idea when he realizes how Zaroff takes the idea to its extreme.

Connell constructs "The Most Dangerous Game" to emphasize the brutality of the worldview that there are only two classes, "the hunters and the hunters." Although Rainsford makes this remark as an almost casual observation, Connell demonstrates how General Zaroff takes this idea to an extreme and why. He suggests that a militaristic and imperialistic mindset facilitates General Zaroff's ruthless disregard for human life. Referred to by his title, General Zaroff alludes to his experience as a military leader on several occasions. As the owner of Ship-Trap Island, General Zaroff also controls the island territory as the landowner and de facto ruler. His relationship with Ivan and his treatment of the men he captures and hunts on the island emphasize how these roles and their associated power dynamics are exploitative. Both because he owns the island and because he controls it, designing its layout, the General has disproportionate power over everyone within it. Even as he insists that he maintains a code of honor, based on his identification as "a gentleman and a sportsman," Rainsford, and thus the reader also, appreciate that this code only reinforces the distinction between the hunter and the hunted.

When General Zaroff pursues Rainsford, perceiving it as both the ultimate honor and challenge because of Rainsford's reputation as a hunter, Connell emphasizes the horrible irony that the General perceives hunting as a game. Rainsford is, of course, afraid for his life; his behavior is that of someone increasingly desperate to survive, aware that if discovered, for example, he will die. When he climbs a tree to escape discovery, for example, he is terrified when the General not only follows his trail but appears to register that he is in the tree. Rainsford even suspects that the General lets him be in this instance only because he enjoys the hunt and wants to extend it across three days. Connell's descriptions of Rainsford's fear reconfigure several earlier allusions to General Zaroff's hunting, too. For example, when the General describes how "[o]ne foolish fellow" tried to escape through "Death Swamp" only to die in quicksand, the reader realizes again how callous the General is to have cared only that the "fellow" made a mistake in the game of hunting, lessening the fun for the hunter, and caused the death of one of the General's dogs.

"The Most Dangerous Game" is, in one sense, a simple story of "cat and house," "hunter and hunted," as the narrative directly states on several occasions. With its careful allusion to historical and social contexts, though, the story offers a complex profile and criticism of societies that maintain imperialistic power structures, allowing those with power to pray on those without. The conclusion in which Rainsford overpowers the General also illustrates the dangers of treating human beings as animals. Rainsford says that he is "still a beast at bay" when he confronts the General, taking on the animal identity into which the General has forced him. This same identity, however, does not register the codes that the General seeks to reinforce. Accepting the role of a hunted animal, Rainsford presumably attacks without waiting for an invitation. The risk of treating humans as animals, then, according to Connell's story, and with allusions, presumably, to the breakdown of hierarchies in World War I, is that they may ultimately rebel by rejecting social codes all together.

The Story of an Hour

by Kate Chopin (1894)

HISTORICAL AND THEMATIC CONTEXT

KATE Chopin, born Katherine O'Flaherty, is perhaps best known for her novella, *The Awakening* (1899), which tells the story of a married woman's sexual awakening. Considered somewhat notorious because of her representation of extramarital affairs and female sexuality, Chopin is celebrated today as a forerunner of American feminist literature.

Of Louisiana Creole heritage, Chopin frequently sets her stories, including "The Story of An Hour," in Louisiana, and incorporates the cultural complexity of this region within her fiction. Her two novels, *At Fault*, published in 1890, and *The Awakening*, are set in New Orleans and the Grand Isle respectively.

Although the Louisiana context is less relevant to "The Story of An Hour," it provides a setting for readers to access and judge what is not being said in the story regarding the rights a woman of that time and place would have within marriage, and the type of cultural expectations on her about how she should react to, and feel about, her husband's passing.

CHARACTER INSIGHTS

Mrs. Louise Mallard is the protagonist of the story, to whose perspective Chopin offers the most substantial and consistent access, Louise Mallard reacts to the apparent death of her husband in the space of an hour. This constitutes the basis for the entire story. From the beginning, though, Chopin implies that Louise is exceptional. Although she is "young with a fair, calm face," she has "lines [that] bespoke repression and even a certain strength." People say that she has "a heart trouble" that necessitates "great care" from those who share the news about Mr. Mallard's apparent death. Informed of the fatal accident by her sister and a family friend, Louise also reacts in an unusual way—"she did not hear the story as many women have heard the same." Rather than experiencing a "paralyzed inability to accept its significance," Louise reacts to the news of her husband's death with "sudden, wild abandonment," which is presumably unusual for a woman with heart issues. She then disappears into her room and reflects on her new freedom. When she emerges from her room, apparently excited to embrace her new life, she dies from the shock of seeing that her husband, in fact, is alive. The sight of him walking through the door is the "joy that kills," with Chopin leveraging the extreme dramatic irony that it is in fact Mrs. Mallard's "joy" at the prospect of a new life that actually causes her to die.

Josephine is Louise Mallard's sister, Josephine attends her sister when a family friend chooses to share the news of Mr. Mallard's death. Josephine embraces her sister as she reacts to the news of Mr. Mallard's death and then is the one to stand outside of Louise's room, calling her by name and encouraging her to emerge.

Richards is a friend of Mr. Mallard, Richards takes it upon himself to inform Mrs. Mallard about her husband's death. To try and ensure that the information is accurate and that he is not causing undue stress, he was "in the newspaper office" when he heard the announcement of the railroad accident. He also sends a second telegram to get confirmation that Mr. Mallard is indeed dead before he goes to Mrs. Mallard. This care and attention suggests that Richards is a diligent friend, however, the reader might also question why it is within a matter of a few hours (at most) that Richards proceeds to summon Josephine, Mrs. Mallard's sister, and goes to Mrs. Mallard himself to tell her that her husband is dead. Railroad accidents are such that it is possible it might take additional time to identify who actually died.

Mr. Mallard, the husband of Louise, the story's chief protagonist, is rumored to have died in a railroad accident. He is an absent presence throughout the story, and his death is the catalyst for the narrative events. Chopin offers the strongest impression of him through the way in which Louise reacts to the news of his death and how others expect her to react. The actions of Richards and Josephine suggest that people believe the Mallards to have a strong relationship—Richards and Josephine apparently expect Louise Mallard to have a violent reaction to the news, such that might endanger her health. Although described as somewhat unusual, Louise does indeed react strongly to the news of her husband's death—she cries a lot in her sister's arms. After her initial outburst of grief, when she contemplates her husband's death, she also appears to acknowledge that she has real feelings for him. She registers that she will miss him. She actually does not feel guilty about being excited at the prospect of her freedom precisely because she knows that she will miss her husband's "kind, tender hands" and "the face that had never looked save with love upon her." Chopin's indirect characterization of Mr. Mallard implies that he was a good husband, but even this is not enough to mitigate the restraint of marriage for a woman.

VOCABULARY RESOURCE

Aquiver—*adjective*; marked by trembling or quivering

Bearing—*noun*; 1. the manner in which one behaves or comports oneself, 2a. the act, power or time of bringing forth offspring or fruit, 2b. a product of bearing, 3a. an object, surface or point that supports, 3b. a machine part in which another part turns or slides, 4a. the horizontal direction of one point with respect to another or to the compass, 4b. a comprehension of one's position, environment, or situation

Bespoke—*adjective*; 1a. custom-made, 1b. dealing in or producing custom-made articles, 2. engaged

Fancy—*verb*; 1. to have a fancy, 2. to believe mistakenly or without evidence
—*noun*; 1a. a liking formed by caprice rather than reason, 1b. amorous fondness, 2. notion, whim, 3. fantastic quality or state
—*adjective*; 1. whimsical, 2. not plain, posh 3a. of particular excellence or highest grade, 3b. impressive

Forestall—*verb*; 1. to exclude, hinder, or prevent (something) by prior occupation or measures, 2. to get ahead of (something), anticipate, 3. to prevent the normal trading in (something) by buying or diverting goods or by persuading people to raise prices, 4. intercept, 5. obstruct, beset (more obsolete usage)

Importunity—*noun*; 1. the quality or state of being importunate, 2. an importunate request or demand

Monstrous—*adjective*; 1. having extraordinary often overwhelming size, 2a. extraordinarily ugly or vicious, 2b. shockingly wrong or ridiculous, 3. deviating greatly from the

natural form or character, 4. very great (used as an intensive word), 5. having the qualities or appearance of a monster, 6. Strange, unnatural (more obsolete usage)
 —*adverb*; very, extremely (example: a monstrous long raft)

Sank—*verb*; past tense of the word sink, 1a. to go to the bottom, 1b. to become partly buried, 2. to fall or drop to a lower place or level, 3. to become deeply absorbed (example: sank into reverie), 4. to go downward in quality, state, or condition, 5. to grow less in amount or worth, 6a. to fall or drop slowly for lack of strength, 6b. to become depressed

SAMPLE ESSAY

In "The Story of An Hour," Kate Chopin explores Louise Mallard's initial reaction to the news that her husband has died in a train accident. Published in 1894, the story is controversial because the central protagonist, a woman, appears enraptured by the news of her husband's death: she experiences an outburst of grief and then retreats to her room, where she begins to embrace with enthusiasm the prospect of being an independent woman. Through "The Story of An Hour," Chopin explores the restraints upon women and emphasizes the damage done by these restraints, suggesting that they can literally kill.

Through the initial character representation, Chopin suggests that Louise Mallard is little understood by those around her. Both her sister and a family friend, Richards, arrive to break the news about Mr. Mallard's apparent death. They determine that she has "heart trouble" and that she must be told carefully to avoid an exacerbation of her position. Despite these concerns, Chopin shows that Louise is actually capable of managing the shock. She displays a slew of emotions, very dramatic in nature: she weeps in a way that is flood-like, her emotions compared to a storm, rapidly affecting her. Yet, once this initial outburst is over, Louise becomes calm. Chopin suggests that Louise's reaction may even be somewhat performative because she is torn between grief and excitement as she begins to process what her husband's death means for her.

Once Louise retires to her bedroom, Chopin reveals that she is very excited about her future. Chopin conceptualizes Louise's excitement through imagery, gesturing to the view out of the window, the blue skies that are opening up, and the approach of spring. Particularly playing with the association between spring and new life, Chopin exploits the irony of Mr. Mallard's apparent death just before the spring season and the way in which Louise Mallard perceives the possibility of new life in the world around her, from the vantage point of her own room. While Louise is this space, realizing her new-found freedom, Chopin also reveals her first name, affirming her identity and suggesting the extent to which her marriage has, although it was never exactly unhappy, retrained her to the point that she lost her individuality.

The final irony of the story, of course, is that Louise dies when her husband walks through the door. The narrative persona declares that her death is from "the joy that kills," with the other characters presumably concluding that Louise Mallard died from the sudden and overwhelming joy of discovering that her husband was alive. Because of different elements within the story to which the reader is privy, though, the narrator's remark is clearly ironic; the reader registers that Louise was happy to be free, although she was not entirely happy that her husband was dead. Indeed, because of the attention that Chopin plays to the guilt that Louise feels about her happiness and relief, they register that she is indeed devastated to discover her husband still living.

The complexity and success of this story both rest on the idea that Louise Mallard can at once love her husband and relish the opportunity to live for herself. The story explores the challenging situation of women in the late nineteenth century, allowing that they may well have meaningful attachments to the men in their lives, including husbands, but they also find themselves at odds with these attachments and with men as representatives of the patriarchy.

The Garden Party

by Katherine Mansfield (1922)

HISTORICAL AND THEMATIC CONTEXT

KATHERINE Mansfield (1888-1923) was born Katherine Beauchamp in New Zealand and grew up in a suburb of Wellington. She traveled to Europe regularly and eventually moved there as an adult. She began writing short fiction, inspired in part by her cousin, Elizabeth von Arnim, who was also a successful writer.

Written in 1922, "The Garden Party" first appeared in serial form as "The Garden-Party." It was published in three parts, in the *Saturday Westminster Gazette* on February 4th and 11th, and then in the *Weekly Westminster Gazette* on February 18th, 1922. Mansfield later included it in her collection, *The Garden Party and Other Stories*, published in 1923.

Like many of Mansfield's stories, "The Garden Party" is set in New Zealand and draws on her experience of growing up in a relatively luxurious house in Thorndon, Wellington. Exploring the way in which the Sheridan family reacts to the news of a young man's death, on the same day that they are giving a garden party, the story displays many elements of modernism. It sometimes adopts a very cinematic style, for example, drawing on the emerging tradition of film. It also emphasizes class differences and related tensions to show the instability of the traditional social structure.

CHARACTER INSIGHTS

Laura Sheridan is the protagonist of the story and Mansfield's narrative mostly aligns with Laura's perspective in the text. Laura belongs to a well-to-do family, presumably based in Wellington, New Zealand, although Mansfield never specifies location. Laura has grown up in relative privilege and appears to only have a passing awareness of the lower-class families that live so close to her own home. Overseeing arrangements for a garden party, though, Laura reacts strongly to the news that a relatively young man—a father and a husband—has died in an accident. She immediately proposes calling off the party because she considers it wrong to continue with a celebration of sorts after such a near tragedy. She is surprised to find herself in conflict with her family—including her mother—on this point. When she later goes to visit the family, taking a basket of food and flowers left over from the party, she is deeply embarrassed but also keenly moved by the experience of seeing death first-hand. Observing the young man, she concludes that he looks if he is asleep and utterly contented, which she finds a revelation.

Mrs. Sheridan is Lauren's mother and appears as a powerful maternal figure. She has several children and takes pleasure in watching their activities. In the context of the story, Mrs. Sheridan encourages her children to plan a party, seeking to give them responsibility for the event. However, she is unable to resist taking over the planning at key points. Being also the moral center of the family, Laura looks to her initially for help when she wants to convince her siblings that they should cancel the garden party. Laura is at least somewhat surprised that Mrs. Sheridan doesn't believe the party should be stopped because of the death.

Jose is Laura's younger sister who disagrees with Laura about whether the party should be called off. Her initial argument with Laura about this sparks the discussion with Mrs. Sheridan, who sides with Jose.

Laurie Sheridan is Laura's brother and the one to whom Laura turns after she visits the Scott family. It is to him that she speaks about the profundity of the experience she has observing the corpse of Mr. Scott.

Mr. Scott is a neighbor of the Sheridans who dies close to the Sheridan's home following an accident. His body is laid out in his home, where Laura visits him and believes that he is sleeping and looking peaceful.

Mrs. Scott is the wife of the dead man and a minor character within the story. She encounters Laura towards the end of the narrative. She is in mourning and aided by her sister.

VOCABULARY RESOURCE

Absurd—*adjective*; 1. ridiculously unreasonable, unsound or incongruous, 2a. having no rational or orderly relationship to human life, 2b. lacking order or value

Beastly—*adjective*; 1a. characteristic of or resembling an animal, 1b. characterized by cruelty, brutality, or crudeness, 2. extremely unpleasant, disagreeable, or undesirable, 3. monstrously large or powerful
   —*adverb*; in an unpleasant or beastly manner

Conspicuous—*adjective*; 1. obvious to the eye or mind, 2. attracting attention, 3. marked by a noticeable violation of good taste

Extravagant—*adjective*; 1a. exceeding the limits of reason or necessity, 1b. lacking in moderation, balance, and restraint, 1c. extremely or excessively elaborate, 2. extremely or unreasonably high in price

Haggard—*adjective*; 1. not tamed, 2a. wild in appearance, 2b. having a worn or emaciated appearance,
   —*noun*; 1. an adult hawk caught wild, 2. an intractable person

Lanky—*adjective*; ungracefully tall and thin

Plume—*noun*; 1. a feature of a bird, 1a. large conspicuous or showy feather(s), 2a. a material worn as an ornament, 2b. a token of honor or prowess, 3. an elongated and usually open and mobile column or band (such as smoke)

Queerly—*adverb*; to do something in an unusual, questionable, strangely, uncomfortably or suspicious manner

Rapturous—*adjective*; 1. to feel ecstasy or passion, 2a. to feel carried away by an overwhelming emotion, 2b. to feel as if you are having a mystical or divine experience

Shied—*verb*; 1. to make a sudden throw, 2. to divert, 3. to avoid

Sordid—*adjective*; 1. marked by baseness or grossness, 2a. dirty, filthy, 2b. wretched, squalid, 3. meanly avaricious

SAMPLE ESSAY

In the short story, "The Garden Party," published in three parts in February 1922, Katherine Mansfield explores the dilemma of Laura Sheridan, who, upon hearing about the death of a young man, questions whether her family should cancel the party that they are hosting. Emphasizing the role of class prejudice, Mansfield establishes the complexity of Laura's moral dilemma, and suggests the enduring tension between life and death.

In the opening lines, Mansfield creates a striking sense of continuity. The first word of the story, "And," suggests that the narrative begins in medias res, with the characters' activity in preparation for the garden party obviously predating the start of the timeline within the text. With this subtle maneuver, Mansfield alludes to the epic dimensions of the story that she is about to tell. The characters within the story are perfectly ordinary, with the Sheridans representing a moderately wealth family and the various workers standing in for the lower classes. The key events of the story—the garden party and the young man's death—are also relatively unexceptional. Mrs. Sheridan complains that young people always want parties, and there is a constant suggestion throughout the text, shortly after the announcement of the man's death, that death is a perfectly common occurrence in the world—this is part of Mrs. Sheridan's justification for continuing with the party. Nevertheless, the scope of the story's themes—the engagement with questions about life and death—imply that it may not actually be a meaningful gesture to cancel the party. After all, Mr. Scott's death is an accident, suggesting that life is unpredictable. The accidental nature of his death also emphasizes how fragile life is, and how inevitable death is.

Laura's appeal to her mother, Mrs. Sheridan, expands the moral dilemma of the story, too. On the one hand, the reader's empathy with Laura, built through the proximity of the narrative proximity to her own, privileges her response. When Laura insists that it is inappropriate to host the party, Mansfield invites the reader to agree; the party sounds like a trivial event and one bound up in class privilege, hosted and attended by those who look down on the working class affected by the tragedy. When Laura clashes with her sister Jose, she immediately turns to her mother, who has the appearance of unwavering maternal authority. Mrs. Sheridan, however, insists that it is unreasonable to cancel the party just because of a tragic event. She suggests that it is unfair to a greater number of people to call off the event, which suggests that there is an emphasis on a kind of utilitarian ethics. Mansfield does not spend much time unpacking the reasoning behind this conclusion, but it is enough that Mrs. Sheridan believes that it would be inappropriate to cancel the party, and she is clearly someone to whom Laura looks up within the family.

Laura's attitude towards the dead man is also difficult to decipher within the story, but her suggestion that life is "marvelous" based on this experience opens a number of possibilities. Here, the adjective connotes something that may be positive or simply overwhelming. It may also indicate something that is strange or unusual. Since Mansfield does not limit her application of the term, it is possible that that she intends the reader to conclude that Laura applies the term in every one of these ways.

By leaving open the moral dilemma of the text and likewise suggesting that Laura perceives something entirely exceptional about the young man's dead body, Mansfield firmly establishes her story as a meditation upon the value of human life. She further suggests that a tension may always exist between the human desire to celebrate life and the need to acknowledge death, although the two processes need not be mutually exclusive.

ADDITIONAL RESOURCES

Semantic Map Example

Semantic Map Sample for "The Most Dangerous Game"

Uniform trimmed with astrakhan photo credit: Soviet Military Stuff

Cossack photo credit: wikicommons images, public domain

Created by: Amelia Emery 2023

Text Insight Endnotes

1   Clearly this is intended as a suggestive name, alluding to the idea that the island is designed to specifically "trap" ships. It is ironic, too, because this is very likely what it does given General Zaroff's design of the island.

2   The environment is critical because it emphasizes an attitude of Western readers towards that which is considered exotic or "other" than Western.

3   Big-game hunting was extremely popular at the time the story was written, but it is predominantly a sport for the white, European and American elites.

4   Rainsford's perspective here will be challenged by his experience on Ship-Trap island.

5   Although Whitney has a very small role, his perspective here is critical as the first challenge to the positive view of hunting that Rainsford initially presents and that General Zaroff takes to extremes.

6   Rainsford tries to dismiss the idea that big-game hunting is anything more than a sport. He rejects the idea that it has moral implications, as Whitney is trying to suggest.

7   This is the critical social view that Connell challenges throughout the story.

8   Cannibalism was almost always associated with native tribes and reviled as a heinous act.

9   This is relatively advanced knowledge for the time period, recognizing that both sound and lights have waves.

10   The choice of location is important here. Situating the story on a Caribbean island, the author at once positions himself to draw on the lore of the sea, since the Caribbean was an important area for sailors (and pirates), and also establishes the story in a relatively remote and exotic location.

11   The suggestion here is either that Rainsford does not focus enough to try and recognize the "animal" sound or he is already suspicious about what is going on and he does not want to know what is going on.

12   Here, the treacherous landscape matches with situation in which Rainsford finds himself. This is clearly a dangerous scenario, with someone firing off a gun in an unknown region. Rainsford's determination to explore shows his bravery, but from the landscape, it is clear that this bravery may be misplaced.

13   The description of General Zaroff emphasizes his "original, almost bizarre quality." "Black" is a notable color in his description, too. His eyes are "black and very bright." He also has a "dark face," suggestive of his aristocratic status. His military background is also suggestive of his authoritarian personality.

14   Cossacks are from southern regions of Russia.

15   The medieval style of the dining room is a nod to the traditional, aristocratic, and authoritarian context of the house.

16   The collection of animals as trophies and specimen emphasize how General Zaroff is a hunter, someone who seeks to dominate the world around him.

17   General Zaroff clearly identifies Rainsford as someone he admires. He shows here that he is also an expert on hunting; in fact, obsessed with it based on all that he has read. That his one passion is "the hunt," however, is also an example of foreshadowing through characterization. This one passion is going to drive the plot and the reader can connect this passion to the mysterious gun shots and the evidence of an animal having been shot.

18 The foregrounding continues here and there is a clear irony in the description. The General indicates that he has to stock his own island for the hunting that he wants to do. The hunting, however, suggests that the whole island is set up for his amusement.

19 The general maintains that his role as a hunter is divinely ordained.

20 This appears to be an allusion to the Russian Revolution. Connecting to the references to the Cossack cavalry and the General's family holdings in the Crimera, the suggestion here is that the General has a dubious background. He may well have been involved in atrocities in the Russian Revolution. As someone who is also in exile, it notable that he isolates himself in a remote location.

21 General Zaroff here appears as a god-like figure and a dictator-type. He establishes this island as veritable play land in which every detail is established for his amusement—"perfect for [his] purposes."

22 Here the author introduces the moral dilemma of the story. The General seeks to amuse himself by hunting men. As Rainsford points out, this is, of course, murder. However, as the General emphasizes, hunting virtually every other kind of animal is allowed, if not actively encouraged in the world they occupy. Because the general perceives humans as animals, he insists that this mitigates any moral dilemma. It is a logical conclusion that he should hunt humans when other kinds of prey no longer challenge him.

23 Here the author also introduces a tension between a practical and logical mindset, and one that is romantic, perceiving human life to be of a particular value.

24 The allusion to the war here provides an important historical context, too. The author uses the war as a context to explain the limited value that General Zaroff—a representative of the military based on his title—attaches to human life. His use of the war as justification here suggests that one of the author's larger points is about the way in which the war has undermined the valuing of human life.

25 Europeans, seeing themselves as belonging to an Old World, are positioned here as more seasoned, more traditional with respect to values. Here, however, the suggestion that Rainsford's attitudes are conservative is a misleading conclusion from the General. Obviously, it is not conservative but a right way of thinking that to kill a human being is morally wrong.

26 Civilized is a loaded term. There is an enduring tension between the idea of what is civilized and what is uncivilized. One of the central themes in this story is undoubtedly what constitutes civilized behavior.

27 General Zaroff reveals here that he is capturing people who run into the rocks near his island. His "training school" models a military establishment, consistent with his title. Given that it is a "cellar," it has clear resonances with a prison. The General's disappointment about the "inferior" quality of the "specimens" also emphasizes how he dehumanizes people and treats them as prey through his use of language, in addition to the actual process of hunting. There is a suggestion of racism here, too, given that the specimen are Spanish.

28 The theme of racism is developed here, too.

29 It is intensely ironic that the General considers himself "a gentleman" in all this, and he invites Rainsford to trust him purely on this basis when he is otherwise imprisoning and murdering people.

30 The general is more concerned about the death of his dog than he is about any of the individuals that he has killed.

31 Rainsford's anxiety and the general's behavior—the comparison of the two to cat and mouse—emphasizes how the General seeks to use psychological warfare.

32 This is another important example of animal imagery.

33 "Madame Butterfly" is a famous opera by Giacoo Puccini in which the heroine commits suicide.

34 Rainsford plays with the issue of animal behavior. By indicating that he is still a "beast at bay," he hints to the General that he intends to behave like an animal, rather than a gentleman or a sportsman (at least in so far as the General seems to understand either role as dependent upon honor). However, whereas the General expects Rainsford to wait, and for there to be a "fair" fight between the two of them, Rainsford clearly does not wait. The last line of the story cuts ahead to show the reader the outcome of the encounter: Rainsford is sleeping in the General's bed, meaning that the General dies. The penultimate paragraph, however, emphasizes how Rainsford confronts the general with his own celebration and practice of animalistic behavior: he invites him to experience the irony of his celebration of animalistic behavior by demonstrating animals will fight to survive.

35   The narrator refers to the central protagonist, Louise Mallard, by her married name until the point at which her apparent "freedom" is obvious. The lack of specificity about the heart disease from which Louise Mallard suffers provides Chopin with scope to play with the idea of how others treat Louise. It is unclear, even at the end of the novel, whether she does really have a heart condition, or whether people around her are just particularly careful of her. Her death, from shock, though dramatic, could also speak to the scope of the surprise that she experiences.

36   The refusal to speak directly to Louise is notable here. Both her sister and the family friend who seek to break the news to her about her husband insist that she must learn about the death indirectly and slowly. The use of "hints" particularly emphasizes that Louise seems childlike or is at least treated as such by those around her.

37   This suggestion is striking given the prominence of the railroad in the 19th century. Here, both the railroad and the technology the telegram are tied to the dramatic change that Louise experiences through the implied loss of her husband. This may be ironic, although it is also a realistic way to suggest that Mr. Mallard died in a disaster.

38   Her exceptionality is emphasized here already. She is an individual and how she reacts to news of her husband's death defies convention. We are perhaps invited to consider who determines the way in which "many women" react to news of their husband's death. Also interesting is the difference between Mrs. Mallard's reaction and that of many women is that she apparently succeeds in understanding its significance while other women, most women, do not. This also begs the question: what is the significance of a husband's death to his wife?

39   This description emphasizes the overflow of emotion that Mrs. Mallard demonstrates. It is interesting to consider how this expression of emotion fits with the idea that she has a weak heart, though. Surely someone with a weak heart would struggle expressing this swell of emotion. It is dramatic, even over the top. Is it genuine?

40   The symbol of the open window is critical. It represents freedom here.

41   Is this exhaustion the result of her expression of emotion or something else? Does Chopin suggest here that marriage is what exhausted Mrs. Mallard?

42   It is critical here that Louise sees the "new spring life" opening up before her as she looks out on the world from a new height. The energy of "spring" also suggests the new vibrancy and new hope that comes with her understanding of her new position as a widow. it is also ironic that Mr. Mallard is supposed to have died in the spring, typically a season of the year associated with new life and rebirth.

43   The sensory language here reinforces the point about new energy and vibrancy.

44   The clearing away of clouds shows how this is an emerging opportunity, as the blue sky again emphasizes freedom and possibility.

45   This is the first acknowledgement of what Louse looks like. It is interesting that she is described as young, because the heart condition, coupled with certain other aspects of her earlier representation might lead the reader to believe that she is older. Also, the mention of repression here is an interesting idea. How is Louise repressed? Is it because of her husband specifically or the idea of marriage? Is it from life in general? The note about her strength also emphasizes her hidden depths and the notion of her abiding potential.

46   This narrative build-up introduces a new kind of tension. It is complicated because of the situation regarding her husband—that he has died. Yet, Chopin suggests that the liberation of Louise, following her husband's death, brings a strange kind of release.

47   Again here Chopin emphasizes the mix of emotions. Louise is clearly ecstatic but also experiencing "terror" at the realization of her own happiness, relief, and freedom. This mix of emotions sets up the conclusion to the story, helping to make it plausible.

48   "Monstrous joy" is an example of paradox that applies for much of the text.

49   This is the heaviest expression of the irony of the story, of course.

50   Mansfield creates an immediate sense of continuity with the choice of "And" to open the story.

51   Mansfield builds a sense of class difference throughout the story, beginning here with the account of how the gardener is working to prepare for the party that will take place later that day.

52 Mansfield indicates the different role played by the Sheridan family members in preparing for the party. Compare the planning work they do to the work of the gardener, for example.

53 The nature of hospitality is an important theme within the story as it connects to the idea of how people treat one another.

54 Mansfield emphasizes class difference here, through use of language. The difference between how the working class characters speak and how the Sheridans speak is one of the techniques used throughout the story.

55 Laura's concern about obscuring natural beauty with the trees is striking as a suggestion that she is perhaps different from her family. She privileges natural beauty.

56 Laura's desire to connect with workmen here perhaps betrays her naivety and her tendency to stereotype the lower-classes, which is certainly indicative of her mother's behavior as well. Considering Laura's desire to connect at least somewhat genuinely, however, further suggests why she is affected by the death of her neighbor more than any other of her relatives. However misguided she may be in her approach, she has the desire and thus the potential to connect with those outside of her own class.

57 The excess of flowers ordered by Mrs. Sheridan suggests her ostentatiousness and her meddling behavior.

58 The initial announcement of this pivotal event makes it seem almost insignificant, and suggests that "the man" was someone unknown.

59 Laura's immediate reaction is that they should stop everything. No one else within the story appears to have this same reaction.

60 The suggestion that it is "absurd" and "extravagant" to stop the party emphasizes the values ascribed to the social scenario, the weight of class difference, and the strange commonality of death. Mansfield never establishes whether Laura is right to suggest that the party should be cancelled, and there is certainly a counterargument to her position, which is that death or otherwise tragic things happen all the time.

61 For Laura, the proximity of the dead man is a key issue.

62 The class difference emerges again as an issue here, now with the emphasis that there is sometime "revolting" and "disgusting" about

the lower-class community so close to the Sheridan's home. The revelation of this detail at this point in the story emphasizes the moral dilemma again, adding to its complexity.

63   The desire to ascribe blame to the man is striking here.

64   It is notable here that Laura expected her mother to react as she does, serving as a moral compass for the rest of the family.

65   With attention to the hat, Mrs. Sheridan seems to try to get Laura to focus on herself.

66   Mrs. Sheridan suggest that there is a balance—a need to prioritize the enjoyment of the majority over the feelings and interests of the few.

67   The emphasis on Laura's beauty here is striking. Her beauty, her status as a "charming girl in the mirror," provides the basis for the continuation of life.

68   Mrs. Sheridan seems to ascribe blame here, insisting that it is only for her children that she deigned to have the party in the first place, when she clearly directed a lot of the festivities and was ultimately the one insisting upon it.

69   The parental discourse here again reiterates the distinction between Laura and her parents but also complicates the representation of Laura's sympathy. She doesn't like being teased; it is difficult to gauge from the tone whether her parents really lack sympathy for the dead man and his family. Mansfield's insistence on complicating the representation is what keeps the true complexity of the moral dilemma in focus.

70   Here, Mansfield emphasizes another key difference between Laura and her mother. Laura is reluctant to take food over to the family of the dead man because she is not sure that it is appropriate, whereas Mrs. Sheridan seems convinced that it is an appropriate, even helpful, move.

71   Even in her apparent gesture of kindness, Mrs. Sheridan is class-conscious.

72   The representation of death as peaceful and a state of happiness is striking here. Laura's interaction with the dead man, apologizing for her hat, emphasizes the oddity of the scene. Is it appropriate

that Laura sees the dead man as happy? Is she right to think that he looks "peaceful" and "content" in death?

73   Mansfield leaves it to the reader to interpret here what exactly Laura's feelings are regarding the encounter with the dead man— "marvelous" is a contentious term. The reader is also left to question to what extent Laurie understands her position, too, given that he struggles to relate earlier.